Self-Publishing Attack!

The 5 Absolutely Unbreakable Laws for Creating Steady Income Publishing Your Own Books

James Scott Bell

#1 Bestselling Writing Coach
Award Winning Thriller Author

c

Compendium Press

ISBN: 978-0-910355-03-2

Compendium Press
P.O. Box 705
Woodland Hills, CA 91365

Also by James Scott Bell

On Writing:

Plot & Structure
Revision & Self-Editing for Publication
The Art of War for Writers
Conflict & Suspense

Fiction:

One More Lie
Watch Your Back
Deceived
Try Dying
Try Darkness
Try Fear
Pay Me in Flesh (as K. Bennett)
The Year of Eating Dangerously (as K. Bennett)
I Ate the Sheriff (as K. Bennett)
City of Angels
Angels Flight
Angel of Mercy
A Greater Glory
A Higher Justice
A Certain Truth
Glimpses of Paradise
No Legal Grounds
The Whole Truth
Presumed Guilty
Sins of the Fathers
Breach of Promise
Deadlock
The Nephilim Seed
Blind Justice
Final Witness
Circumstantial Evidence
The Darwin Conspiracy

ACKNOWLEDGMENTS

Grateful acknowledgement is made to the following people for help in the preparation of this book: Kristin Billerbeck, Stephanie Higgins, Kelly Long, Jim Rubart, Jen Jones, Sharon Dunn, Marlo Schalesky, Lyn Cote, Donita K. Paul, Robin Caroll, Kristen Heitzmann, Tamara Leigh, Tom Morrisey, Sibella Giorello, Bob Elmer, Rick Acker, Randy Ingermanson, Brad Whittington, Janice Thompson, Trish Perry, Jill Nelson

Table of Contents

Part One: The Dream - It Begins 1

Part Two: The Laws 27

Law #1: You Must Think LIke a Publisher...................... 29

Law #2: You must Write the Best Books You Can.......... 41

Law #3: You Must Prepare Your Book With Quality Controls... 65

Law #4: You Must Develop and Work a Marketing Plan 97

Law #5: You Must Repeat Over and Over For the Rest of Your Life 124

About the Author 128

PART ONE: THE DREAM

He felt that his whole life was some kind of dream and he sometimes wondered whose it was and whether they were enjoying it.

Douglas Adams, *The Hitchhiker's Guide to the Galaxy*

It Begins

One day in the merry month of May I noticed my bank account was larger than it had been the day before.

I immediately thought of Monopoly. "Bank Error in Your Favor. Collect $200."

Only this was more than $200.

Looking into it I saw that I'd received a direct deposit from Amazon and their Kindle Direct Publishing program.

I called out to my wife.

She wasn't there. I was in the house alone. That's usually the case because I'm writing and my wife is out in the real world doing something of great value and being with actual people. People who are not tied down to a keyboard, monitor and chair calling out to people who aren't in the house.

So I called her on the phone and gave her the good news. Because she was part of the reason it had come.

I was one of those holdouts for the romance of the physical, printed book. I love books, always have. I have shelves and shelves of them (like many dedicated readers, I can hardly bear to give my books away).

Most of my life has been spent with books--reading, toting, collecting and traveling with them.

When we got married, I told my wife she'd have to be willing to go into any used bookstore we happened to walk by in any city we visited. She was fine with that, as she loves books, too.

But then for Christmas, 2010, Cindy got me a Kindle.

There it was, in my hands, this nifty but controversial little device. I say controversial because many were calling it a weapon of destruction. Death to books! Death to print! Death to a great industry called publishing!

Maybe I was thinking this a little bit, too.

But when I started to download...

Suddenly, I had the complete (complete!) works of Jack London, for $2.99.

I was studying the Civil War at the time and saw that the

two-volume, Pulitzer Prize winning history of the war by James Ford Rhodes, published in 1918, was available . . .again, for $2.99!

Astonishing, incredible, fabulous, wonderful.

Then there was the amazing Project Gutenberg online-- thousands of classics in the public domain, free for download. In Kindle format! I got several books I'd long wanted to read, like Theodore Dreiser's *Jennie Gerhardt* and Edward Bulwer-Lytton's *The Last Days of Pompeii*.

And they cost me zip.

There were new books, too, by writers I already followed, like Dean Koontz and Michael Connelly. I paid "normal" prices for these ebooks and I had them *now*. I didn't have to drive to a bookstore or wait for the UPS guy.

And when I traveled, I didn't have to stuff a couple of paperbacks into my carry-on. I had a virtual library with me inside the Kindle . . . not to mention Mine Sweeper and Sudoku.

Also a boatload of samples that I could browse at my leisure.

Hog heaven, as they say, especially for an ex-ham like me.

Yes, the Kindle was indeed a game changer. And I knew there was no turning back or stemming the tsunami that was heading for the publishing industry.

I'd also been reading about the authors who were jumping into indie publishing in a big way.

People like J. A. Konrath and Bob Mayer and Barry Eisler. In fact, the big news just coming in was that Mr. Eisler had turned down a $500,000, two-book contract from St. Martins to go completely indie!

Things were, to put it mildly, getting interesting.

Traditionally published authors were champing at the bit to put out their own ebooks, though some were getting blowback from their publishers. (One author, in fact, had come out with a series of short stories in the same genre as her full length books. Her publisher went ballistic, cancelled her contract and sued her to get the advance back. Wow).

As someone who loves to write, the prospect of putting out more product, fast, and getting paid directly for it, was too much to pass up.

So I put out my first, self-published ebook, *Watch Your Back,* a novella of suspense and three short stories. I priced it at $2.99.

The first full month it was available it sold 920 copies in the domestic Kindle store.

And I thought, *Hmm, maybe a writer can make some real lettuce at this thing.*

I set out to figure the best way to do that, to test what I was doing, study others who were doing it well, keep notes on everything and, finally and most importantly, do it myself in actual practice.

I have, and this book is the result.

****

I am going to assume throughout that you want to know how to do it yourself (DIY). There are, of course, self-publishing services that offer some attractive benefits. BookBaby and BookTango, for example. And new ones coming along all the time. If you go that route, read the fine print, compare, and get recommendations. Take your time.

There is Smashwords, a one-stop distribution service (or you can pick and choose which ones you want Smashwords to handle). Many authors choose to create accounts directly with Amazon and Barnes & Noble and go through Smashwords for the rest.

As an advanced option, you can also set up your own store at your website.

The point is, you have many choices.

Choices are nice things to have.

You may already be self-publishing. If so, I want to help you keep on doing it and doing it even more successfully.

Now, if you think self-publishing is a road to getting rich

quick, disabuse yourself of that notion immediately. In the early days of the indie revolution, authors who jumped in with backlist titles certainly managed to clean up nicely. But the gold rush days are over.

You cannot realistically expect that you're going to put one book out there and rake in enough to buy a summer home in Malibu.

The name of the game is to learn how to make a steadily growing income from self-publishing. It's possible. More possible for a writer than at any time in history.

The Old Days and Old Ways are Over

Back in the old days, and by the old days I refer to those days prior to November 19, 2007 (the day the Kindle went on sale), and stretching back to approximately 3024 BC, it was very difficult for a freelance writer to make a living at his trade.

If you worked incredibly hard and managed to cultivate some reliable clients — meaning editors at magazines — you could perhaps eke out a minor subsistence writing things you thought were right for certain markets.

Most of your time would be taken up with research on periodicals that buy articles on subjects you find moderately interesting. You'd even take on something you *didn't* find interesting if you could sell it.

In short, you would constantly be trying to find things that would reach a paying market and then when you did, you would sell one-time rights and receive a minor stipend and that was that.

There was really no life after the article was published.
I think it was S.J. Perelman who said, "The dubious privilege of a freelance writer is he's given the freedom to starve anywhere."

If you were a writer of fiction, the prospects were even more dire. In the old days, you had to land an agent and then a book contract which brought you an advance, and then you had to sell enough books to earn back that advance for the publisher. Then you would get royalties. But most novels fail to take off, and the number of people who were able to actually make a living writing fiction could dance with angels on the head of a pin.

In those days, self-publishing was looked at as the final act of a drowning, desperate writer. On rare occasions––about the same number of times a meteor dropped on Ames, Iowa––a self published book would catch fire. It wouldn't take long for a traditional publisher to swoop in and buy up those rights, giving a lump of money to the author but keeping most of the net income ever after.

That's because, as I said earlier, the only way to really distribute a print book was if a big publisher took you on. They were the only ones who could get you into bookstores. They were the only ones who could produce a book that looked halfway decent. It was the only game in town.

And for most writers, it felt like the Forbidden City was

surrounded by impregnable walls.

The bottom line was there was no real bottom line for those who wanted to write for a living. Especially if it was fiction that floated the writer's boat. Most writers suffered through years of rejection and many never made it past the walls.

They went to their graves leaving behind boxes of manuscripts that never sold and scattered dreams that were never realized.

Some were bitter. Some even turn to desperate marketing measures:

"Rich are the records . . . with stories of penniless authors, who, sick with hope so long deferred, and at last despairing, have resorted to wild and tragic devices . . ."

So begins a story in the *Los Angeles Examiner*, New Year's Eve edition, 1905. The feature tells the tale of one such anguished author, a school teacher named Edith Allonby. For four years she'd labored on a novel, *The Fulfilment* [that's the correct spelling] into which she poured heart and soul. She had been published before, but her books had not been hits. *The Fulfilment* was going to change all that. In fact, Miss Allonby thought its spiritual themes would change the world.

But the book was rejected. First, by her own publisher. Then by all the other publishing houses she sent it to. "I have submitted my book to all these men," she wrote in a note. "I have tried in vain. They will not accept it, yet shall

'The Fulfilment' reach the people to whom I appeal, for I have found another way."

After finishing the note, Miss Allonby changed into a silk evening gown, put fresh flowers in her hair, and sat in a comfortable chair. She was found dead the next day, her manuscript on her lap and an empty bottle of carbolic acid at her side.

This is not a career move I recommend.

Even though book was published the following year (and soon went out of print).

But such was the lot of writers in the old days. Unless a writer was admitted into the Forbidden City, there was no hope, no chance . . . and no dollars. (In a twist of sweet irony, *The Fulfilment* is now available as an ebook and will be, presumably, forever).

Still, there were benefits to the freelance life:

1. You could be freed from punching a clock
2. You could make your own hours and dress how you like
3. You could choose your work environment
4. You couldn't get fired
5. You could decide what projects you wanted to pursue

Well, these are the same benefits a self-published writer making a five-figure income can realize as well.

There were also downsides to the freelance life:

1. No benefits
2. Sketchy paydays
3. Ups and downs of the market
4. Tax and accounting responsibilities

And these, too, are part of the five-figure income self-publisher's life. But they can be handled with a modicum of effort.

I think the benefits of true freelance writing were summed up in the title of my favorite book on the subject: *Too Lazy to Work, Too Nervous to Steal* (by John Clausen). The cover of the book featured shoes propped up on a desk.

Which has always been my ideal working position.

When I was just starting out, the Mac was starting out too. I remember an Apple magazine ad showing a guy in his penthouse apartment, wearing a sweater and slacks, his feet up on the table, his cat in his lap, his Mac at his side. He was working.

I cut that ad out so I could look at it from time to time.

Later, I found a picture of one of my favorite authors, Stephen King, working in his home, leaning back in a chair with his feet on his desk and his manuscript on his lap.

I still have that picture in my office.

In other words, I was putting those images in my mind so I could realize the same lifestyle someday. And I did. I was one of the lucky ones who was able to make a living doing the kind of writing I loved.

Now, with self-publishing, I can see how many more writers than ever before will have that same chance. The opportunities are vastly greater now than at any time in the history of the written word.

The "bad old days" when writers had only a thin hope of ever reaping substantial lettuce from their efforts are gone. It's possible, if you are disciplined and consistent and have a modicum of talent, to realize a good return on your writing. Like a five-figure return. Every year. For the rest of your life.

The purpose of this book is to help you get there.

A New Definition of Writing Success

When we talk about self-publishing and the idea of "success," we have to define our terms. When I first got started in self-publishing I was under two traditional publishing contracts. I had no complaints. I was being paid well, my books were selling steadily, and I received nice royalty income.

So while money was certainly a motivation ("No man but a blockhead ever wrote anything except for money," wrote the inimitable Samuel Johnson) it was not the sole or even the most important one.

Most important to me was freedom. I always wanted to publish more than I was able to in the traditional world. So success in self-publishing meant that I was producing more work, selling it directly to readers, and making a steady stream of income from it.

Here is a clip from a blog post I wrote in January of 2012:

We all know the traditional model is shrinking. Advances on new contracts are at historic lows. With physical shelf-space disappearing, print revenues are down. And while digital income is up for the publishers, the slice of that pie given to most authors remains stagnant at 25% of net.

Still, many writers remain focused on traditional. It represents some sort of "validation" even though it could very well mean less income (the right circle) over time.

But now a new model of writing success has appeared. Writers, for the first time since the troubadour era (when you could go out on your own and make up stories in song and get some coins for it), have it within their power to get their writing out without a middleman (the fancy term is "disintermediation").

And further, unlike self-published authors of yore, they actually have a chance to make some real money doing it. Every day, we are hearing more accounts of self-published writers who are earning significant income as independents.

The new model looks like this:

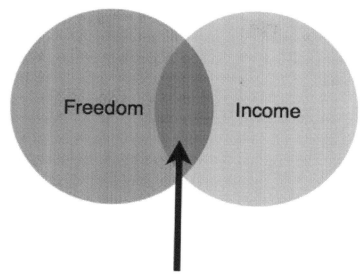

The New Zone of Success

Freedom is an invaluable commodity. To be able to write what you truly want to write, and know that you can get it into the marketplace, is tremendously freeing. It is, in fact, the engine of happiness for a writer. It's exhilarating to write for yourself, see what you've written, fix it, and keep on writing—and then to be assured that it has a place in the stream of commerce, for as long as you live.

I can tell you I've never been more jazzed about being in the publishing game than I am now. Not just because of increased production and income, but because of the freedom to take responsibility for my own work.

Let me be quick to point out, however, that this responsibility carries challenges. Being in charge means you are CEO of your own publishing enterprise. You can expect to experience the stresses and strains of running a small business. You will need new skills to handle them. These can be acquired, but only through effort and self-discipline.

But it's more than worth it to be fully in charge of your writing and your life. It's tremendously freeing, exciting and so doggone *fast*. I love seeing something I've written and edited make its appearance within a matter of weeks. I love getting paid every month. I love this whole new world of possibilities for tellers of tales.

Now, it's true that I had a readership when I started self-publishing. But I purposely went slow because I wanted to experiment and see what I could do that was repeatable. I wanted to study others who have done it right.

I wanted to be able to lay down some rules and "laws" for long term success.

Let's start with the things you'll need to develop in order to lay a foundation for gaining a profit from your labors.

What You Will Need to Succeed

An Entrepreneurial Spirit

If you are going to self-publish, you are going into business. You need to think, act and plan like a business.

This requires the spirit of the entrepreneur, the risk taker, the business builder.

The nice thing is that self-publishing requires very little up front financing. You don't have to worry about renting a storefront or office space or hiring staff or getting business insurance.

But you do have to hire yourself. That's what you're doing, in essence.

What you have, though, is what all the great entrepreneurs have enjoyed--freedom. To make your own way with your own brainpower and work ethic.

I still believe that's a dream worth pursuing.

And if you are going into this as a career path, and are serious about following the 5 Laws, I strongly encourage you to create an actual publishing company and incorporate. My company, Compendium Press, is a subchapter S corporation. It's incredibly simple to do this. You can use a service like LegalZoom.com to set it all up.

While it's not necessary to incorporate as a solo author, there are advantages to it, not the least of which is it forces you to think like business.

Self-Discipline

There are three things that are required for success as a writer: talent, luck, discipline … Discipline is the one that you have to focus on controlling, and you just

have to hope and trust in the other two. — Michael Chabon

There are three aspects of self-discipline you must master to be the best you can be. They are: Goal setting, time management and action.

1. Goal Setting

I believe that *written goals* are foundational in any kind of ultimate success. While it is certainly possible to reach some achievements without them, you can go even further, faster, if you are purposeful about setting goals-- and writing them down for review.

It is therefore crucially important to distinguish between dreams and goals.

A dream is something that creates a picture in your mind. It's an ideal that can motivate you to action.

For example, a writer might dream of being on the *New York Times* bestseller list. He can "see" his name in print there. He can "see" people congratulating him.

But he cannot make it happen. He cannot control the outcome.

What can he do?

He can set concrete goals that he *can* control.

Such as:

a. Spend two hours per week studying the craft of writing.

b. Write a certain number of words per week.

c. Read three novels a month in his genre.

d. Become a member of a critique group within the next three months.

e. Attend one writing conference per year.

f. Produce one novella and a short story by December 1.

Notice that each one of those goals has a time element attached to it. That way, you can actually measure when you have reached, or not reached, your goal. A time element gives you "positive pressure," which is what a good entrepreneur needs.

And if you don't reach a goal, you analyze why not and set a new goal.

Try this: write down a list of ten goals. Just brainstorm them. What can *you* do within a certain time period (say, the next six months) to get further along your path?

After you've come up with the list, re-prioritize it. Concentrate on your top five.

Next, and most important, you must create a plan of action for each goal. This is important so you can actually take steps toward achieving your goal, and make adjustments along the way.

For example, let's say your goal is to complete your novel by December 1. It is now June 15.

Write your goal (I like handwriting these, as there just seems to be another physical connection to the brain that way) and put it into an "I will" statement: *I will complete the first draft of my novel, THE UNBEARABLE LIGHTNESS OF BEING GERALDO, by December 1.*

Now break that down into an action plan. Let's say you've got 58,000 words to go to reach an 80,000 word goal. You've got 168 days to do them. Divide 58,000 by 168 and you come up with 345.238095 words per day. Make sure you do exactly that each day by typing a partial word at the end of your writing stint.

Kidding.

Round up to 346 per day. Since I advocate a weekly quota, with one day off per week, I'd make part of the plan 2,076 per week. That is easy to measure. Thus:

    a.   I will write 2,076 words per week.

You also know that your work schedule will get hairy, and finding time to write will be a challenge. Another part of the plan might be:

b. I will wake up one hour earlier than normal, make coffee, and type 300 words before I do anything else.

c. Maybe you know you're going to have some uninterrupted time coming soon. Vacation days. The use of a friend's mountain cabin.

d. From August 6 – 9 I will write for five hours a day, each day, and complete at least 800 words each day.

So there is your first goal and plan, written out. Maybe your second goal is: *I will read and study one new craft book a month for six months.*

a. Research the top rated fiction craft books in an online store

b. Pick six books you want to read

c. Buy the books

a. d Create highlights and notes from each book

d. Create your own writing exercises to practice what you're learning

e. Apply the techniques to your current Work-in-Progress (WIP)

Taking time to set goals (and write them down!) is a major factor separating those who succeed from those who dawdle.

Write them down and read them each day. When you do that, and take action, it creates in you a feeling of being unstoppable. And that's a great feeling to have.

2. Time Management

The second part of self-discipline is managing your time. Oh, it would be nice to frolic, like the Eloi in *The Time Machine,* never worrying about where the time went. But then you'd get eaten by Morlocks.

We have a finite amount of time on this orb and we need to make the best use of it. Especially if we want to generate consistent income from self-publishing.

Time management principles are basic:

> a.   Plan in advance
> b.   Write it down
> c.   Prioritize
> d.   Eliminate obstacles

Plan in advance by looking at your week and deciding what things you need to do in that span. Write them all down. Generate a long list of items.

Then go through those items and put them in A B C order.

A is for those things you *must* do that week.
B is for items you'd *like* to do that week.
C is for those things that can *wait* until another week.

Then go through the As and put *them* in priority order.

A1
A2
A3

Put a time estimate for each one. Let's say A1 is getting a new laptop, which you desperately need. You have already researched your options and know what you want and know the store where you're going to get it. The store is about fifteen minutes away. You estimate an hour at the store. So you put 1.5 next to A1.

And so on through your list.

Now, look at your work week (on a weekly calendar) and find the spots to place all your As. If you can work in your top Bs, do that, too.

Forget about the Cs.

And there's your week. Once you get used to this system it doesn't take long at all. I suggest planning your weeks on Sunday. Then you have an action plan for the entire week.

It saves a whole lot of wondering-what-to-do-next time.

3. Action

The final step in self-discipline is the most important. That is translating goals into action.

Without action, nothing else on these lists matters.

For a writer, that means writing and studying the craft. Robert A. Heinlein, the famous science fiction writer, once gave out his bottom line rules for writers:

1. You must write

2. You must finish what you write

Pretty hard to argue with that.

Which brings me to the single most important piece of writing advice I ever got: establish *a quota system.*

Listen to what one of the most prolific novelists of his time did while working full time for the British postal service. Anthony Trollope (1815 – 1882) says in his autobiography:

"There was no day on which it was my positive duty to write for the publishers, as it was my duty to write reports for the Post Office. I was free to be idle if I pleased. But as I had made up my mind to undertake this second profession I found it to be expedient to bind myself by certain self-imposed laws. When I have commenced a new book, I have always prepared a diary, divided into weeks, and carried it on for the period which I have allowed myself for the completion of the work. In this I have entered, day by day, the number of pages I have written, so that if, at any time, I have slipped into idleness for a day or two, the record of that idleness has been there, staring me in the face and demanding of me increased labor so that the deficiency might be supplied."

The daily recording of the number of words you write is an invaluable incentive to get your work done. But set your goals on a weekly basis, as Trollope did. "According to the circumstances of the time—whether my other business might be then heavy or light, or whether the book I was writing was or was not wanted with speed—I have allotted myself so many pages a week."

My suggestion is that you find a comfortable quota, one you can easily meet, then start meeting it. After a few weeks, if you've been successful, raise it by 10%.

Review your quota every six months or so. Try to keep it challenging but reachable.

You will be amazed at the results.

Talent

Of all the characteristics a successful writer needs, talent is near the bottom.

That's what I said.

The number of literary geniuses no one's ever heard of is too great to count. That's because it takes more than talent to get anywhere, in any field. You have to have the aforementioned self-discipline, for one thing. And a lot of years of practice.

Yes, you have to be able to use the English language.

Yes, you have to know how to string sentences together.

And yes, you have to be able to stir up your imagination and get new stuff out of it.

But those things can be learned.

The key is to tap into yourself and bring out the gold.

Brenda Ueland, author of *If You Want to Write,* said, "Everybody is talented, original and has something important to say. Everybody is talented because everybody who is human has something to express. Everybody is original if he tells the truth, if he speaks from himself. So work with all your intelligence and love. Work freely and rollickingly, as though talking to a friend. Mentally (at least three or four times a day) thumb your nose at the know-it-alls, jeerers, critics and doubters. Work from now on, until you die, with real love and imagination and intelligence. If you are going to write you must become aware of the richness in you and come to believe in it and know it is there."

If you are worried about your talent or how to get it to show, I suggest you read Natalie Goldberg's *Writing Down the Bones.*

A Social Network

I know many people are afraid of social media, the time commitment, the uncertainty of the ROI (return on investment).

Relax. It's not as hard as you think, nor is it as make-or-break as you imagine. It's necessary in this world, but if you follow a few simple guidelines your online life will be much easier.

See the section on social media under Law #4 for specifics, but you can start laying the groundwork now.

Establish a footprint in social media, and you can take more steps as you go along.

Perseverance

Indie author Mark Young (*Revenge, Off the Grid*) says: "I'd like to caution new authors that it is not a walk in the park. Sometimes the effort can be very challenging because you feel you are out there doing it all by yourself with no safety net. And, you are going to face those who want to criticize you as having 'taken the easy route' without submitting your work to traditional publisher and agents for their concurrence that you have what it takes. Whether a writer chooses the traditional publishing path or the self-publishing path, they must believe in themselves. For those who go the indie route, I think their self-confidence will be sorely tested. Hang in there. Believe in yourself."

Your Mileage Will Vary

Many authors are liberal in sharing their sales and income numbers. I'm not one of them. Only on rare occasions, for illustrative purposes, have I given out this information (such as the item about my income that began this book). The reason I don't hand out more on this matter is that such information is pretty much meaningless.

No one can replicate another author's record. No one. Each author and body of work is unique. Innumerable factors play into the results, many of which are totally out of the control of the author.

So there is really no point in putting up numbers. If you're intent on making money publishing ebooks, you can do it. Even your cat can do it. So can your ficus.

It's easy to make a profit publishing ebooks, as long as you realize that profit may only buy you a Starbucks once a month. Nothing wrong with that. But you probably want more.

The way you'll get more is to follow the five laws given in this book.

Listen: *It is the very best time to be a writer. There is more opportunity to make real dough from books than has ever existed, anywhere, anytime.*

The world is now the writer's oyster.

Let's step up to the oyster bar.

PART TWO: THE LAWS

It is found by experience that admirable laws and right precedents have their origin in the misdeeds of others.

Tacitus

Law #1: You Must Think Like a Publisher

The biggest challenge faced by self-published authors, it's not marketing, it's not discoverability, it's adopting the best practices of the very best publishers. It's about becoming a professional publisher. – Mark Coker, CEO, Smashwords (in Digital Book World, May 8, 2012)

There are three main functions of a publisher: acquisitions, production and marketing. Everything a publisher does falls under one of these umbrellas.

You therefore need to understand what these functions are and begin to apply them to your own book.

Yes, just as if you were a business publishing the books of

someone else.

Acquisitions

A publisher needs product. It needs to keep acquiring new product. It needs to keep the stream flowing.

To do so, it goes through an acquisitions process.

Let's take a look at how it usually goes at a traditional publishing house.

An editor receives a book proposal, usually from a literary agent. If the editor likes the proposal, she may ask to see more of the manuscript or decide to sell the book based on the proposal itself.

Yes, the editor must sell the book to a committee. The publishing house committee includes someone from sales and marketing. That's the team that must be sold on a project, for they are the ones who are going to try to sell it to bookstores.

That's a simplified view, and there may be various in-house hoops the editor has to jump through (including a numbers crunching sales analysis, which is bad news for a writer whose books have not had great sales success in the past).

Once the committee accepts the project, the editor begins the negotiation process with the agent.

So what is the editor looking for?

1. A book that will make money

2. A book that will make money

3. A fresh and exciting new voice

4. And a writer who can keep writing books that will make money

You should be thinking exactly the same way. You want to write books that are fresh and exciting to *you*, and you want to do this over and over.

And you want them to make money.

Only you can make the decision of what kind of book to write. But it's no sin to write in a genre that is popular and doesn't conflict with your conscience.

I'd advise you to first look at the genres you love to read.

For me, I like thrillers. Fortunately, that's one of the most popular genres. I made that decision based on what I like to read.

Other writers go into it with money making as the supreme motivator. Nicholas Sparks is up front that this is what he did. He was looking at the bestselling genres and determined there was room for two authors to dominate any list.

All the genres were taken, except one: short, tear-inducing fiction written primarily for women by a male author. That's because it was new, led by *The Bridges of Madison County* by Robert James Waller.

So that's the market Sparks aimed for, and he hit it big.

What are the most popular genres?

- Romance
- Thrillers
- Paranormal
- Speculative/Fantasy
- Historical
- Mystery

You can mix and match these, too. For example, when zombie fiction started to take off I pitched an idea to my agent about combining zombies with legal thrillers. He went out and sold the Mallory Caine, Zombie-at-Law series to Kensington (written under the pseudonym K. Bennett).

Series can also do very well in ebook form. Here's a nasty little secret about traditionally published series: virtually all of them tail off. That is, the subsequent books in the series usually sell fewer and fewer.

Of course, there are exceptions. A series can "hit" and sell hugely. Ever heard of Harry Potter? Harry Bosch? (There's a key for you. Create a series character named Harry. Kidding!)

Janet Evanovich and Sue Grafton and Robert B. Parker didn't do so bad with series characters.

But they are in the minority.

That is, where traditional publishing is concerned.

For indie publishers, creating a series character may help spur sales. That's because the point of entry into a series is less costly than in the traditional world.

There, if you wanted to get caught up in, say, a six book series, you'd be spending a lot of money and time.

But ebooks, with their lower price point (and an astute author may price the first in the series very low to get readers hooked) and instant delivery, are much better suited for gaining new readers all along the life of the series.

Another nice thing about genres is that, as a self-publisher, you can experiment around. This brings up the issue of "branding," which I blogged about at Kill Zone. Here's a clip:

Back in the "old days" *branding* was a key concept in the traditional publishing world. Still is, actually. That's because a publisher trying to make money with an author has to build a readership, and that's done over time, book by book. Readers who become fans expect that new books by the author will be similar in tone and genre to the ones they've enjoyed.

Take a hypothetical author. Let's call him Gil Johnstrap. He comes out with a terrific first novel, a thriller about a boy on the run from the law. A fan base starts to form and they eagerly await his next book. If that book were to be about a horticulture competition in Surrey, England, circa 1849, they would tend to be confused and frustrated. They might decide to skip the next Johnstrap because they're not sure what it contains.

So Gil and his publisher come out with another thriller, this one about a family on the run from the FBI. Fans buy it and are happy. They start spreading the word to other thriller fans about this Johnstrap fellow. The growing base looks forward to the next thriller. And so it goes.

Now, if an author becomes overwhelmingly popular, like a King, Grisham or Patterson, they earn the right to try, on occasion, something "off brand." King might write about a girl lost in the woods. Grisham about a painted house. Patterson about whatever the heck he wants—I have a feeling his parking tickets would sell a million copies.

But the publishers will insist on getting "back on brand" with the next book, because that is the bread and butter for them, the guaranteed sales.

Cut to: today. And e-publishing. What is the state of branding now? Let me start with my own experience.

I have been writing contemporary suspense, like the Ty Buchanan series for Hachette and *Deceived* for Zondervan. I've augmented those books with novella/story collections I've self-published. These all fall into the suspense category, so they are complementary.

I've self-published a couple of boxing stories, because I like writing them. And they bring in nice-dinner-with-my-wife money each month.

I write zombie legal thrillers under the pen name K. Bennett for Kensington. I plan to augment these with short, paranormal stories. These stories will make new readers for the novels, so both publisher and author win.

As mentioned up top, I'm re-launching a historical romance series, six books in all.

I daresay the readers of the Kit Shannon books may find the Mallory Caine, Zombie-at-Law books a tad "off brand." But that's okay. Two different audiences, but with potential cross-over.

I also do non-fiction for Writer's Digest Books. And I have some non-fiction ideas I plan to self-publish.

So here's the question: Can I do it? Can an author today juggle several brands?

My answer: Why the heck not?

Branding in the days of print-only was partially determined by physical shelf space and seasonal purchases. An author could not come out with several different titles at roughly the same time. Bookstores wouldn't buy. And they'd be a bit confused. If Gil Johnstrap did write that horticulture novel, *A Garden in My*

Heart, would it be placed on the thriller shelf next to his other titles, where fans would look? Or on the romance shelf? Or in "Gardening"?

But there are no such limitations in the digital world. All books are "shelved" cover out. Digitized books are given, via algorithm, space next to similar books. A reader can find new authors in a genre this way. Quite easily.

An author can distinguish between his brands via cover art, book description, tagging, and even a pseudonym.

John Locke, poster boy for self-publishing success (Note: This was written before the news that Mr. Locke paid for Amazon reviews was made public. I have decided nonetheless to keep what I think will be of value, despite the source), writes contemporary thrillers and Westerns. Like Robert B. Parker did after he became a household name with Spenser.

As I said a couple of years ago, the new e-publishing era is a lot like the old pulp fiction days. I look back at a Depression-era writer like Robert E. Howard. He wrote stories in the fantasy, horror, detective, western and boxing genres. All of 'em. That can be done again, right now, in today's world. It's a great time to be a writer who loves to write.

There is only one fly in this ointment: a traditional publishing contract with a non-compete clause the publisher is determined to enforce. I know some writers in this predicament. And while I understand that publishers are undergoing paradigm shock right now, this is not the best option. They should be willing to re-negotiate these clauses so writers can earn some extra income and make new readers without harming the brand the publisher wants to create.

It can be done. It should be done.

So I see no reason why writers cannot be stretching and experimenting and flat-out having fun writing whatever kind of material excites them and complements a strategic plan for their careers. Even if it means different brands.

John "One Million Ebooks" Locke, writes, "If you want more readers than you can get by writing to your niche, you'll need to create a second stream of income — a DIFFERENT niche. That's why I created my western series of Emmett Love novels. It's a whole different niche. I can build a separate loyal audience for that series without screwing up the Creed franchise." *(How I Sold 1 Million ebooks in 5 Months!)*

So don't restrict yourself to one brand if you're passionate about other genres.

Make a list of your favorite genres and match that with the kind of book you want to write. The more passion you feel for your writing, the better it's going to be, so choose wisely.

But here's the nice part: you can always go another direction, too.

Another suggestion I'll make is this: write short form as

well as long form. You can put short stories out there, too. In fact, do enough of them, and you can add new content and collect all those stories into one volume and sell it.

For example, you put out four, five or six short stories. Sell them for 99¢.

Don't expect to break the bank on those stories. But eventually you can bundle them, add a novella or more stories, and go back to market again with them, priced, say, at $2.99.

Production

The second key area in publishing is the production aspect.

In the old days, quality production was only achieved within the walls of the Forbidden City. Only there was the quality editing, design, print and distribution system. No self-publishing author could possibly compete with that and still have money left over to live on.

And, in fact, production is what traditional publishers did very, very well.

Think of the 1950s mass market paperback revolution. Remember those racy, provocative but ultimately irresistible covers? Those were rendered by talented artists working away for publishing companies who could afford to pay them.

And then there were all the layout matters, the printing and binding, the multiple decisions that were involved in every single book brought to market.

A quality production system is at the heart of traditional publishing. That heart is, unfortunately, getting strained at the moment. The rise of ebooks, the loss of physical shelf space and brick-and-mortar stores, the cutting of editorial staff in favor of digital marketing staff, have all presented cracks in the walls of the Forbidden City.

Which is one reason many traditionally published authors have turned their backs on that city and gone into the indie forest to dwell with an ever growing band of Merry Authors. They ask, if I am still being offered the same old terms but getting less of the same services, why shouldn't I go directly to readers?

So, quality production. That is a system you are going to have to develop for yourself if you want to go indie. More on that later.

Marketing

The final step, of course, is marketing. Publishers have to sell these great products.

That's never been an easy thing to do. If it were, every book published would become a bestseller.
There is an old saying: We know that 20% of marketing works. We just don't know which 20%.

Later in the book we'll talk about what you can do to market your own works. For now I'll say that if you learn to think like a publisher, you'll start to do the following:

1. Spend your time developing the books you want to write most, but which also have the potential to sell to a large audience.

2. Make sure all the aspects of the book, from editing to cover design, are top quality. In a 2012 survey of over 1,000 self-published writers, the website Talelist concluded that, "self-publishers who received help (paid or unpaid) with story editing, copy editing and proofreading made 13% more than the average; help with cover design upped earnings by a further 34%."

3. Develop a marketing plan and work your plan.

Let's look at how to write a great book that sells.

Law #2: You Must Write the Best Books You Can

Okay, this seems like a no-brainer, right?

Wrong.

The landscape is littered with the digital flotsam and jetsam of lousy books tossed out there too soon.

There is still only one sure-fire way to sell books, lots of books, over a period of years: word of mouth.

That means people read your books and like them so much they talk about them.

"Eighty percent of your book's success will be determined by the quality of your book. The other 20 percent is distribution, marketing and luck."(Mark Coker, *The Secrets to Ebook Publishing Success*)

Yes, you'll hear this over and over again. You'll see it on blogs and in ebooks about how to sell ebooks.

But here I want to offer you some actual advice on *how* to become a better writer, and *how* to write better books.

Both fiction and non-fiction.

If you want to add to your streams of income, you'll consider both.

And learn to do both well.

FICTION

Leonard Bishop, in *Dare to be a Great Writer*, said, "Dramatic characters, inventive plotlines, exciting and intense situations are not achieved through accident or good luck. The writers of great books zealously learn the craft of their profession so they can release the power and depth of their imagination and experience."

You can learn to write fiction.

I wrote a whole book, *Plot & Structure*, in order to destroy what I call The Big Lie: that writers are born, not made, and no one can learn the craft and become a better writer of fiction.

Bunk and baloney on rye with mustard.

I've taught tens of thousands of people—through my books, seminars, workshops, mentoring clinics and at conferences—and have lost count of the numbers who've credited me with taking their fiction to the next level. Many have gone on to get publishing contracts.

Critically acclaimed novelist Sarah Pekkanen was even kind enough to credit me, Stephen King and Donald Maass, with her success. I like being in that company. It makes me smile, not for the name recognition but because it helps put a stake through the heart of the Big Lie.

A complete education in fiction writing is, of course, beyond the subject matter of this book. But I will give you some guidelines to help you plan for improvement for the purpose of selling more self-published fiction over your lifetime.

Here is what you do:

1. If you're just beginning

Take six months to load up on the kind of book you love to read and want to write. Read with a critical eye, asking yourself questions, such as:

- Why do I care (or not care) about this story?
- What is it about the characters that grabs (or does not grab) me?
- What does the author do to make me read on?
- How does the author begin and end scenes?
- At the end of the book, how do I feel?

And so on. At the same time, be systematically studying books on the craft of writing. Again, if you're just beginning, let me recommend the following books:

- *Plot & Structure* by James Scott Bell
- *Writing Fiction for Dummies* by Randy Ingermanson & Peter Economy
- *Techniques of the Selling Writer* by Dwight Swain

Be systematic about this reading. Every time you learn something, try to apply it to what you are currently writing.

Which is the last thing I'll mention for you. Make sure you have set yourself a quota of words to complete every week. Set the quota on what you can realistically accomplish.

If you have a day job, write early morning or in the evening. Maybe set apart a slot of time on the weekend.

I don't care if it's 300 words or 3000 or 30000. Just find a number you can reach and reach it every week.

2. If you're beyond a beginner

Even if you are experienced writing fiction, you must develop an ongoing improvement program. Your program should include a subscription to *Writer's Digest* and a study of writing books.

Highlight your writing books and review the highlights periodically.

Continue to read, not only in your genre, but in others as well. Read non-fiction, too, as a way of growing your capacity for handling material.

Ray Bradbury counsels fiction writers to read some poetry each day, to expand your language and style capabilities.

If you recognize a weakness in your writing, design a self-study to address it.

For example, years ago I knew I was a good plotter, but I needed to improve my character work. So I did the following:

- I wrote down my goals for the self-study program.

- I took down half a dozen of my writing books that dealt with characters.

- I selected half a dozen novels I remembered liking, primarily because of the great characters in the story. I re-read these with a particular eye toward how I was being drawn in by the characters.

- I took six weeks to go over all the material and practice what I was learning, or re-learning, by writing scenes utilizing the techniques.

This self-study is an empowering thing to do. You can always improve, and you have a way to go about it now.

Finally, consider a critique group. The benefits of a small, dedicated group of writers are several. Novelist Jack

Cavanaugh says, "Not until I joined a critique group did I begin writing for publication. The monthly meetings gave me a deadline, exposure to critique (which made me try harder to prove them wrong), and put me in contact with people who shared a common goal as well as information about publishers' guidelines and needs. If it had not been for the critique group I may never have started writing seriously."

The experience wasn't the same for Robin Lee Hatcher. "I participated in a critique group around books 10 and 11. It was a horrid experience for me. I don't do well writing by committee, and since I am an intuitive writer, I work best without other input during the creative process. With rare exceptions, my editor is the first person who sees the book. Occasionally I will ask a trusted writer friend to read a scene or a chapter if I'm struggling with something, just to make sure I'm conveying what I hope to convey."

If you need that extra push, a critique group can help. But make sure the following factors apply:

- Look for people you have a rapport with. Previous relationships help.

- Keep the group small. Four to seven, give or take.

- Give as much as you get. Make sure you give adequate time to everyone else.

- Establish realistic deadlines and stick to them.
- Make sure the people in the group understand the genre you're writing in.

- Build trust. Check egos at the door.

- Be aware of the envy question. It happens. If someone's writing takes off, it is going to cause some strain. Best to talk about this up front.

3. Some things to keep in mind regarding ebooks

Reading attention spans are getting lower, and the distraction element is getting higher.

That means grabbing the reader and keeping her turning pages (clicking pages? Swiping pages?) is more important than ever.

Your first paragraph has to hook the reader.

Your next paragraph has to dig the hook in deeper.

Every scene needs to have conflict and tension. Yes, every scene.

That doesn't mean gunfire or car chases. But it does mean something that is upsetting the status quo.

In every scene.

Readers are going to be sampling, for free, your opening pages. So do not warm up your engines.

Learn to identify the intersection of your unique voice and vision with the commercial aspects.

Is all of this work?

Yes it is.

You are in business. The publishing business.

And to run a successful business, you must work hard. There is a lot of competition out there for readers' attention.

Give them a good product, a good story, a fictional dream, and you'll create repeat customers.

That's what this business is all about.

4. Before you write it, pitch it

You are not ready to write your novel until you can pitch it in an elevator.

The elevator pitch is the name given to a short summation of the essential plot. Enough so that, if you happened to be on an elevator with a famous director and he asked you about your story, you could sum it up before you reached your destination.

I'm going to give you a simple formula for doing that.

Ready?

First Sentence: Your character's name, vocation and initial situation:

Will Connelly is an associate at a prestigious San Francisco law firm, handling high level merger negotiations between computer companies.

Now do your own. I'll wait.

Second Sentence: "When" + first doorway of no return

The "doorway of no return" is taken from my book, *Plot & Structure*. It's the break away from the first act into the second, into the meat of the story. It's called the doorway of no return because, in a properly structured novel, once the Lead goes through he can't go back to his normal life again. He has to confront the trouble of act two.

Here's our example, continued:

When Will celebrates by picking up a Russian woman at a club, he finds himself at the mercy of a ring of small-time Russian mobsters with designs on the top-secret NSA computer chip Will's client is developing.

Okay, your turn.

Third Sentence: "Now" + death overhanging

By death, I mean the stakes of the novel. They have to involve death.

Death can be of three types: physical, professional, psychological (spiritual). That's how it's got to feel for the Lead. (For a complete explanation you may see my book, *Revision & Self-Editing,* though you should be able to pick up the essence of the concept now).

Our example:

Now, with the Russian mob, the SEC and the Department of Justice all after him, Will has to find a way to save his professional life and his own skin before the wrong people get the technology for mass destruction.

Here's another elevator pitch:

Dorothy Gale is a farm girl who dreams of getting out of Kansas to a land far, far away, where she and her dog will be safe from the likes of town busybody Miss Gulch.

When a twister hits the farm, Dorothy is transported to a land of strange creatures and at least one wicked witch who wants to kill her.

Now, with the help of three unlikely friends, Dorothy must find a way to destroy the wicked witch so the great wizard will send her back home.

At the bare minimum you must have a strong elevator pitch before you write your novel.

As an added bonus, you will use this pitch when putting together your marketing copy for the book. More on that later.

NON-FICTION

To sell a non-fiction book in the "old days" you had to be a recognized expert with a huge platform.

This made sense in the traditional publishing world. The publisher needed to be assured the book would sell.

A book on dog training by Joe Doakes, who was going to buy that?

But a book on dog training by Oprah Winfrey or Courtney Cox or Brad Pitt? Now there's a seller.

Because they have a platform. They are able to get on *The Today Show* or *Good Morning, America*. They do interviews in major newspapers.

If the book was written by a guy who'd made a name for himself as, say, the dog trainer to the stars, then he'd generate enough publicity and endorsements to make the book worthwhile.

Today, you're still going to have to find your audience, but you no longer need a platform *to get published*.

And you are free to write about any subject that interests you, that you think you can sell.

But to do it right, you need to . . .wait for it . . . think like a publisher.

Which means, before you write the book, you should do up a book proposal just like you would if you were trying to sell to a traditional publisher.

In brief, here's how you do it:

1. Create a non-fiction elevator pitch

Just like with the novel, you need to create a winning elevator pitch. Here's how in three paragraphs:

The Most Gripping Question + The Specific Answer

What does every man secretly desire? The ability to kick any other man's butt.

In [Title] You'll Learn + Bullet Point Benefits

In *How to Kick Any Man's Butt* you'll learn...

- *The key to victory in any street fighting situation*
- *The 7 best take down moves*
- *The Chuck Norris secret for ultimate confidence*

About the Author (who the hell are you?)

Joe Doakes was a bouncer and bartender in New York's Hell's Kitchen before joining the Navy SEALs. He has been teaching street fighting for over 20 years. His list of clients includes Brad Pitt, Barack Obama and Richard Simmons.

2. Do a competitive analysis

A traditional publisher wants to know what other books on your subject have been done before.

Doing this helps you enormously, because you can start to figure out how to make your book different. You can find what's called a Unique Selling Proposition (USP) and use it to position yourself in the marketplace.

Such an analysis is easy to do. Just go to Amazon or Barnes & Noble and start poking around.

For our hypothetical kick butt book, I went to Amazon and searched for "self defense."

The first title that came up was *The Dirty Dozen: 12 Nasty Fighting Techniques For Any Self-Defense.* Gotta love that title. That's thinking like a marketer.

And here's the description:

U.S. Army Special Forces veteran Larry Jordan was given a unique assignment by his commanders - come up with a truly down-and-dirty hand-to-hand fighting system for his fellow Green Berets and U.S. Army Rangers. The goal of this system was to give soldiers a handful of hard-core techniques that could be easily learned, easily mastered and effectively applied in any close-combat situation. Jordan devised a set of 12 techniques that were surprisingly simple, shockingly fast and brutally effective. He has now adapted this military system for civilian self-defense. He calls it "The Dirty Dozen." The 12 self-defense lessons in this book are specifically designed to provide the average citizen with a series of easily learned techniques that will enable him or her to prevail in any violent situation. Besides the ever-present threat of violent crime, the recent terrorist attacks aboard commercial airliners show that people can no longer rely on "somebody else" to protect them. Preparing to resist and defeat evildoers is everyone's responsibility now. That's where The Dirty Dozen comes in.

On the book page, of course, is Amazon's "Customers Who Bought This Item Also Bought" algorithm. Here I picked up more books and descriptions.

From there I analyze and attempt to discern where my book can be unique.

3. Develop a preliminary marketing plan

How are you going to reach people that might buy your book? Start brainstorming a plan. This would include:

a. Starting a blog
b. Creating a social media profile
c. Finding top blogs on your topic where you can participate in comments
d. Thinking of possible "influencers" who might be willing to mention your book to their networks

4. Write well!

You have to know how to write, and the best book on that subject is *On Writing Well* by William Zinsser.

Get it. Read it. Study it.

Then write.

Two other titles for your consideration:

Book Proposals That Sell by Terry Whalin
How to Write a Book Proposal by Michael Larsen

The Editing Process

In the traditional publishing world there are (ideally) three layers of editing.

1. Developmental edit. This is a "big picture" view, a look at the overall. Big things, like whether the plot is working, the characters properly motivated and so on. Some of my best books were the result of getting to work with an experienced, talented developmental editor.

Max Perkins was such an editor. He worked with Hemingway, Fitzgerald and Thomas Wolfe.

Bennett Cerf was such an editor. He worked with Faulkner, John O'Hara, James Michener and Ayn Rand.

These days, however, cutbacks in staff have made such editors a very rare commodity for the writer.

2. Line edit. Here, the editor looks for consistency. Does any part contradict another part? For instance, does the Lead character have green eyes in chapter one and brown eyes in chapter twelve?

3. Copy edit. Going line by line to check for grammatical and spelling errors.

Often, the copy edit and line edit are combined.

The developmental edit is the most important and requires the most expertise. Great developmental editors are rare. I've had the great good fortune to work with some and their input was invaluable. But these days, the expense for self-publishing authors may not be justifiable. As an alternative, you can nurture a group of "beta readers" (defined below).

Publishing companies used to make their reputations on the developmental editors they had in-house. Authors who have been through that process have an advantage.

Novelist Brett Battles, now publishing independently, says, "I have a copy editor/proofreader who I trust very much, and who does a light story edit as she's going through it. If anything big jumps out, we stop everything and I fix it before she continues. So I rely a lot on my own instincts and on her keeping me from making major mistakes. Going through the editing process at Bantam Dell for five books helped me a lot in seeing things and being tough on myself. I often feel like I have my old editor in my head. People who haven't had the New York editing experience definitely need to have, at the very least, excellent beta readers who aren't afraid of pointing out issues . . . but would be best serviced by hiring a freelance editor with a good reputation. It may cost good money, but it is well worth it."

If you are new to the editing process you must (I emphasize *must*):

    a.   hire a good, reputable developmental editor or

    b.   find alternative ways to get roughly the same input

Here's the bad news: a good freelance developmental editor, if you can actually find a good one, is going to cost you in the neighborhood of $5000. That can be a little less or a little more, depending.

Why so much? Because this is a specialized area and you pay for what you get. (I have often been approached and asked if I provide developmental editing, and reluctantly I say *Yes*. Reluctantly, because I have to charge so much and I know most writers are strapped for funds. So I usually encourage them to explore alternative b).

So what is the alternative?

Informed, collective feedback.

This is what you would get from a good critique group (another thing that's hard to find) or a group of "beta readers."

Beta readers are those people you have identified as having a good eye for story (fiction) or content (non-fiction). These are friends and friends-of-friends, a network.

What you ask, simply, is that they read your work and

give you specific feedback. The more specific the better. While they will not be able to give you the *fixes* a good developmental editor can suggest, they can identify your weak areas. Then you can take it upon yourself to find the solutions.

For example, if six people read your novel and four of them say they don't like your main character, you have a problem to fix.

If three say they don't get why Sylvia went into the haunted mansion in the first place, you need to check on Sylvia.

If you're writing a how-to book on fly fishing, and two out of six of your readers are confused about your casting advice, you'll need to figure out how to make it clearer.

And so on.

To find good beta readers, make a list of possibles and start asking. Be clear that you are asking them to read and evaluate, not just read and give a one-line response.

Tell them you will put their name in the Acknowledgments section of your book.

Tell them you will insist on giving them a gift in return. What sort of gift? A gift basket from an online store or a Starbucks card.

Don't skimp on the gift.

Think of it this way: if you gift 6 beta readers with 6 gifts with a value of $50, you've spent $300 on a developmental edit. As opposed to $5000.

Further, you can begin to weed out those whose feedback wasn't valuable to you, and add others.

Over time your team of beta readers will become stronger.

Another alternative to a good, freelance developmental editor is a reputable service, like the 2nd Draft service from Writer's Digest.

When it comes to copy and line editing, you really do need to pay for another set of trained eyes. You should not pay more than roughly $2/page for this (assuming standard format, double spaced 8.5 x 11 pages).

Victoria Strauss (http://www.victoriastrauss.com) on the Writer Beware blog (May 3, 2012), offers some excellent bullet points for vetting potential editors (used with permission):

- Be sure the editor (or editors, if it's an editing service) is qualified. You're looking for professional publishing industry experience — preferably, as an editor for reputable publishers — and/or professional writing credentials (legitimately-published books, articles, etc.). If the editor has a website, a resume or CV should be posted there. An editing service should post staff names and biographies. Be wary if you can't find this information, or if requesting it produces excuses or obfuscation.

- Also, for individual editors, membership in the Editorial Freelancers Association (US), the Society of Freelance Editors and Proofreaders (UK), the Institute of Professional Editors (Australia), or the Editors' Association of Canada are all indications of professionalism. (The websites of these organizations provide a lot of helpful information, including sample agreements and charts of recommended rates).

- If you've been referred to the editor or editing service, verify that they're independent. No third party (such as a literary agent or publisher) should benefit.

- Be sure the editor you're thinking of hiring has experience appropriate to your work. Editing is not a one-size-fits-all proposition. Good editors specialize, both on the basis of experience and taste. Someone whose main work has been with nonfiction may not be the ideal choice to edit your epic fantasy novel.

- Look for a client list, or a list of published books. Clients' work published by recognizable publishers suggests that the editor has professional expertise and standing. If the editor or editing service specializes in self-published authors, get hold of a couple of the books so you can assess quality.

- Ask for references and contact them. This is important for obvious reasons.

- Ask to see a sample critique or part of a sample edit. Not all editors may be willing to provide this, but if they do, it'll give you an idea of what you'll be getting for your money. Some editors or editing services have sample critiques on their websites.

- Make sure the business arrangements are clear — and get it in writing. You should know exactly what you'll be paying for, including the scope of the work to be done, the charges you'll incur, the time period involved, and who will be doing the editing (you don't want to pay for a well-known editor only to discover that your manuscript is being handled by an underling). This is important not just for you, but for your editor, who needs to be clear on what you want the edit to accomplish. You should receive a contract or a letter/email of agreement that covers all these areas. Be wary if the editor is unwilling to provide this.

The All Important First Few Pages

In the ebook world, your first pages take on a greater importance than ever before. That's because of sampling. A busy browser who downloads your sample is going to make up his mind pretty quickly on whether to keep going and get the whole book.

This goes for fiction and non-fiction as well.

While it is beyond the scope of this book to dwell on how to write opening chapters that grab, I will give you one simple guideline: start with *story.*

What that means for a fiction writer is this. Begin with action, a real scene, a character in motion. Do not drag us down with what's called narrative summary.

Laguna Beach, California, is a sleepy little town by the ocean. It boasts many amenities of the laid back California lifestyle, and Dominick Corvaisis liked that very much. It was where he had come to heal from a past he wanted to forget.

And he was doing nicely at that. He had become active in the community and was considering running for city council. At thirty-five, he was lean and fit and was finding success as a novelist. But when he started sleepwalking, things began to get disturbing. He did not like it all, this somnambulism.

That's what we in the trade call *narrative summary.* There is no "on the screen" action. It's *telling* us what happened in the past.

It is not story.

Begin with story, the way Dean Koontz does in *Strangers:*

1.
Laguna Beach, California

Dominick Corvaisis went to sleep under a light wool blanket and a crisp white sheet, sprawled alone in his

bed, but he woke elsewhere--in the darkness at the back of the large foyer closet, behind concealing coats and jackets. He was curled in the fetal position. His hands were squeezed into tight fists. The muscles in his neck and arms ached from the tension of a bad though unremembered dream.

And we're off.

See the difference?

Grab the readers from page one . . .with story.

Non-fiction writers, do the exact same thing. Do not begin with a lecture. Begin with a story.

The great public speakers, preachers, teachers and salespeople all know that a story gains the listeners' attention like nothing else.

Don't do this:

In this book I am going to give you dozens of business tips to help you. I will explain to you why certain people are successful at what they do. People like Ted Koppel and Billy Graham and Mario Cuomo.

This book is about being successful in whatever you do!

Bleh. That's stuff for marketing copy.

So how should you begin? The way Harvey Mackay did in his mega bestselling book *Swim with the Sharks Without*

Being Eaten Alive:

The fifteen minutes of fame that the late Andy Warhol promised each of us came to me in the spring of 1984. I was the point man in a nationally publicized effort to outflank Calvin Griffith, the owner of the Minnesota Twins baseball team. Griffith wanted to sell his ball club to a group of Florida businesspeople who would have moved the Twins to Tampa. Another group, consisting of Twin cities people, with which I was involved, wanted to keep the club there, under local ownership--and see to it that we didn't get caught up in a very expensive bidding war.

Isn't that much more compelling? Here you have a high stakes business battle being laid out. It becomes an illustration of the worth of the principles Mackay champions in the book.

That is what you, the non-fiction writer, should do.

In fact, whenever I teach fiction workshops, I encourage non-fiction writers to join in, because more and more of the bestselling non-fiction titles use fiction techniques to keep things moving.

To sum up, editing is where you as a self-published writer can expect to spend most of your up front money. This is your investment in quality and is worth every cent. Because the sum total of your success will be determined by the aggregate quality of your products.

Similarly, skimping on quality will result in the opposite

effect of what you're after: reader retention and repetition. Obey the law!

Law #3: You Must Prepare Your Book With Quality Controls

Here we come to the actual production of your book, getting it ready to toddle off into the schoolyard with all the other books. You want it prepped right and ready to go. You don't want bullies beating it up.

Every successful business knows the necessity of quality controls. As Brian Tracy puts it, "The companies with the highest quality are the companies that earn the highest profits. They represent the greatest opportunities for the future."

Remember, you are in business, and you need a checklist for the essential quality factors for your book production.

Here it is:

Marketing Copy

Marketing copy (sometimes called cover copy or book description) is what you use to entice readers to take a chance on your book. And that's a good way to think about it. Every time a reader plunks down money on a book, she's taking a chance. This is true even if the author is a known quantity. Not every book is a home run.

So each time out you must be about convincing that reader to part with discretionary cash.

The key to understanding marketing copy is that it is *sequential*. What you want to do is grab a browser and move them along to the point where they will want to sample or purchase your book.

Every part of the copy must move the browser to the next part.

The nice thing is most of your work is done. Your elevator pitch is your marketing copy. All you have to do now is add two things: a headline and an About the Author squib. If you have received a blurb from a well-known author or, in the case of non-fiction, an expert in the field, you can add that as well.

Headline

Think of your headline as the hook, the grabber, the tease. A good headline is short, intriguing and captures the essence of the book.

Not something you just dash off. You need a method. And I'm here to give it to you.

FICTION

For a novel or story, you need an adjective, noun and verb.

Let's start with the *noun.*

That is what your character is, her job or vocation. What does your character do? Is she a lawyer, doctor, cop, mother, model?

Name it.

Next, add an adjective/phrase that describes her a little more fully. What *kind* of lawyer, doctor, cop, mother, etc.?

- *Insecure cop*
- *Criminal lawyer*
- *Overworked mother*
- *Aging model*

Finally, the verb phrase, which talks about the main action of the main plot.

For my novelette about a vigilante nun who uses street fighting to battle the criminal element (*Force of Habit*) I came up with the following:

A vigilante nun cleans up the streets of Los Angeles. Sinners beware.

NON-FICTION

To come up with a headline for your non-fiction title, think of the one primary takeaway value for that book.

One. And only one.

You can use the "How to" headline, always popular:

How to feed a family of seventeen on $400 or less a month

How to drive a golf ball over 250 yards every time

How to negotiate anything in ten easy steps

Or something with keys, secrets, techniques and so on:

The keys to staying fit and trim for the rest of your life

Learn the communications secrets of the greatest conversationalists of all time

Of course, not all non-fiction is "how to." There are biographies, philosophical and spiritual tomes, memoirs, investigative reporting and so on.

You can find a headline for each if you just give it some thought and remember your target audience.

For a biography of Sam Snead, you would keep golf fans in mind.

He had the sweetest swing of all time. And he was feared.

If epistemology is your thing:

How do you know what you know?

Investigative:

The newspapers buried this story. Now it returns from the grave.

Have fun with this. Brainstorm. Try things out. Write several headlines in rapid succession and tweak the best ones. Ask several friends which one they like best. Test marketing a headline need not be expensive.

The Copy

The all important book description, or "back cover copy," is your ticket to sales. It's crucially important.

If it looks sloppy or unprofessional, you'll lose sales.

If it doesn't get to the "sizzle" right away, you'll lose sales.

If it's too long, you'll lose sales.

If it's too short, you'll lose sales.

Fortunately, there's a way to make it just right.

Your elevator pitch. You've done all the hard work on that, now you can use it to sell your book.

Let's take a look at examples from both fiction and non-fiction.

FICTION

For *Force of Habit*, since my main character is summed up in the headline, I dove right into the storyline. I added a blurb I've received and finished off with a little embellishment.

When a nun is viciously attacked, Sister Justicia takes it upon herself to find out what happened. The cops don't like that. Neither does her Mother Superior at St. Cecelia's. But when a couple of hoods try to stick up a liquor store and Sister J brings them down, something is unleashed inside her...something that will either confirm her calling...or destroy it.

From "one of the best writers out there, bar none" (Library Review) comes the start of a new series featuring a heroine unlike any other in crime fiction— Sister Justicia Marie, rogue nun.

If criminals are the knuckles, she is the ruler. So be good.

I also write paranormal fiction under the pen name K. Bennett. For my series of zombie legal thrillers with Kensington, the copywriter they hired to do the marketing copy was top notch. He captured the tone of the books superbly. For book #3 in the series, *I Ate the Sheriff*, here is the headline:

Justice. It's what's for dinner.

And the copy:

What's worse than killing a cop? Eating him afterwards. Which is exactly what happened to a Los Angeles County sheriff on Mulholland Drive. Now Mallory Caine, zombie at law, faces the toughest trial of her life - her own - since she's the prime suspect. Ironically, Mallory's been suppressing her undead desires in a 12-step zombie recovery group. It's her human desires that scare her. He's one hot werewolf named Steve Ravener, and he's Mallory's latest client. His ex-wife wants to keep his kids away from him, and if he hopes to see them again, he needs a lawyer whose bite is worse than his bark. Needless to say, family law has never been this hairy. And with a murder charge hanging over her head, a snake goddess charming her mother, and all kinds of hell-spawn taking over L.A., Mallory's plate is full. And she's dying to take a bite.

NON-FICTION

The key to doing non-fiction copy is to stress the benefits and Unique Selling Proposition (USP). Again, your elevator pitch is the copy you'll use.

Here is an example from a book published by McGraw-Hill titled, *How to Talk to Anyone: 92 Little Tricks for Big Success in Relationships.*

Notice how the sub-title itself is a selling phrase, too. Remember that for your non-fiction title! (It's no accident, the subtitle of this very tome you're reading now).

Here are the headline and benefits copy of the aforementioned book:

Become a master communicator and succeed in life, love, and business

Have you ever admired those successful people who seem to have it all? You see them chatting confidently at parties and being listened to in business meetings. They're the ones with the best jobs, nicest parties, and most interesting friends.

But wait a minute. They're not necessarily smarter than you or even better looking. What it comes down to is their more skillful way of communicating with other people. Now *How to Talk to Anyone* reveals the secrets of successful communication. With Leil Lowndes's ninety-two easy and effective techniques, you will discover how to become a master communicator in life, love, and business.

Combining the latest research with Leil's trademark wit and warm-hearted observations of human foibles, *How to Talk to Anyone* shows you how to:

- Make an unforgettable entrance and meet the people you want to meet
- Sound like an insider in any crowd, no matter how little you have in common
- Use body language to captivate audiences of all sizes
- Work a party the way a politician works a room

- **Always come across confident, credible, and charismatic wherever you are**

How to Talk to Anyone, **which is an update of her popular book, Talking the Winner's Way (see the 5-star reviews of the latter) is based on solid research about techniques that work!**

Notice the use of bullet points to get across the benefits. It makes the copy easy to read and accomplishes the sequential strategy we discussed earlier.

Take your time with the headline and the copy. Give it several iterations and get feedback from people. And note that it doesn't have to be long. People have shorter attention spans these days and you want to do what the old time advertising guys used to say: *Sell the sizzle, not the steak.*

Your copy is the sizzle. The first taste of steak is going to be the sample that's downloaded. That's where you close the sale.

Your book description will also include an "About the Author" section. What do you put in there when you're just starting out?

Whatever is relevant.

And don't be cute about it. Unless you are writing humor (and there's nothing harder than writing humor) don't yuk it up. If you've written a thriller, don't say things like this: *Joe Doakes has been called the "next Harlan Coben" by his Uncle*

Ralph, who reads a lot of thrillers.

Readers hate that. They're going to think you're out to scam them.

Just put in material relating to the book, and leave it at that. If you're a lawyer and you've written your first legal thriller, then: *Joe Doakes has been a practicing lawyer in San Francisco for the past 12 years.*

When you start to gather more credits as a writer, or join writers' organizations of note, you can include those: *Joe Doakes is the author of three previous novels in the Geraldo the Avenger series. He is a member of International Thriller Writers and Mystery Writers of America.*

The Comparison Controversy

Should you put in your copy things like: *For readers who love James Patterson and Stephen King?*

Some say that using this will draw readers who are searching for those names, and some magic algorithm will get James Patterson fans over to your book page.

Others say this is baloney.

I lean toward the view that it should not be done. Why? Because most readers are cynical about it. If an unknown author is comparing himself to one of the bestselling writers in the world, that's obvious puffery. The reader is going to be thinking, "Yeah. Sure. Uh-huh." They will be suspicious of your abilities and perhaps distrust you just a little bit. Which is a hindrance when you're trying to close a sale.

What's the real selling point going to be?

Once again, your first chapter.

Front and Back Matter

In a print book, front matter is all the stuff that comes before the body of the work. Title page, copyright page, blurbs, dedication, preface, contents, acknowledgement (sometimes), table of contents. This became the standard. My own early ebooks were done in the traditional manner. This was a mistake.

In the ebook world, we have to think more strategically because of *sampling.* That is, readers increasingly download a sample of the book before deciding to buy it. And if a great deal of the sample is taken up by front matter, readers will get annoyed. Especially if a bunch of it is marketing jazz: blurb after blurb, for example.

Don't do it.

Give the readers what will make them actually want to buy the rest of the book: a good, healthy sample that grabs and does not let go.

I've done my front matter several ways. Here is a simple template I've come up with that I like for future works.

1. *Title Page.* This would be the title, author. Do not put

"by" in there. That's amateur hour. It should look like this:

Watch Your Back

James Scott Bell

2. *Elevator Pitch and copyright notice.* See the previous chapter on the fundamentals of the elevator pitch. Why place it here in the front matter of a book? Because many readers download a bunch of samples for reading later. They can easily forget what it was that drew them to sample your book. This short summary will remind them, and whet their appetite.

This is the place to put one or two blurbs, if you have them. Keep it all on the same page. Consider this a one-page selling document.

For *Angels Flight*, Book 2 in The Trials of Kit Shannon series (still in development as of this writing), my page looks like this:

With her first trial a dramatic success, Kit Shannon steps out from the protective and guiding hand of her mentor and begins her own law practice. When she is drawn to the defense of a man accused of a crime that crosses racial lines, Kit is unprepared for the prejudice and hatred that is hurled in her direction. A loyal supporter of the law, Kit struggles with the secret role of the very officers who claim to represent justice. When a new suitor enters her life, Kit finds her heart longing to embrace the love he offers. His gentle care for her provides the support she needs as she faces opposition

that continually grows more threatening. Could this be God's leading hand?

"Peterson and Bell have crafted another highly suspenseful novel. It will definitely keep you asking, 'What really happened?' and the courtroom scenes are some of the best in the book. Kit is, as always, an inspiring female character with admirable convictions and enviable smarts." – Amazon reader review

Published by Compendium Press

P.O. Box 705

Woodland Hills, CA 91365

3. *Table of Contents.* Usually this comes right before the first page of the main text. However, some authors are putting the TOC in the back of the book, to keep it "out of the way" of the opening. After all, you can click to the TOC from within the book itself and it doesn't matter where it's located. For fiction, this might be an option. But for non-fiction, it should stay up front as part of the sample. Non-

fiction readers make decisions partly based on the TOC.

And that's it. Get right into your pages after that. You are giving readers what they want, a good healthy sample to make an informed buying decision.

Back matter refers to everything that comes after your book has ended. This is where you can do some "up selling" (getting readers to take a flyer on more of your books, if you have them).

But don't overdo this! Readers do not want to feel like a large portion of the book they've bought is given over to advertising. Here is what I would suggest:

1. *Dedication and acknowledgements.* If you want to dedicate the book to someone, do it here (if you want it in the front matter, work it onto the Title Page). Definitely thank everyone who helped you with the book, but do it back here.

2. *Other books.* If you have other titles available, this is the spot to place them with their elevator pitches. Don't go overboard, though. Stick to similar titles. Also, link to your website and author page on the applicable e-stributor platform (e.g., Amazon's page listing all your works).

3. *About the Author.* Optional. A short, strut-your-stuff paragraph if you like.

And there you have it. Keeping it simple and streamlined. Don't pack in too much other "buy my stuff" stuff. People know when you're overstaying your welcome, and it doesn't take much.

As Mickey Spillane once put it nicely: "Your first chapter sells your book. Your last chapter sells your next book." Never has that been truer than now.

Categories, keywords and tags

The online bookstores allow you to categorize your books and put in appropriate key words to help searches. These help browsers find your books. They are important to have, but not obsess over.

A category is a broad umbrella for your type of book.

A keyword is something that helps with searches.

Tags are added after the fact when the books are for sale.

Kindle Direct Publishing (KDP), for example, allows an author to select two categories for a book and seven key words/terms to go along with those.

My novelette, *Force of Habit,* is categorized this way:

FICTION > Mystery & Detective > Women Sleuths
FICTION > Urban Life

My key words are: crime novels, Los Angeles fiction, nuns, martial arts fiction, noir, suspense, action thrillers.

There are two terms that are very specific: *Los Angeles fiction* and *martial arts fiction.* If someone searches for those, the book will tend to be higher in the results.

The more general keywords, like *noir* and *suspense* are there to cast a wider swath, though that puts me in competition with many more titles.

I don't obsess over keywords. I advise you take some time to think them through but know this: they are not going to be the make or break factor for the long term success of your book.

Tagging is something readers can add to your book's sales page, and others can come along and affirm. If you want to see what the most popular tags are, Google "Amazon tag cloud" and follow the link.

Again, no obsession. The most important "tag" is going to be from readers, reviews and sales.

Those, in turn, are going to come from the quality of your book.

Law #2 is the antidote to misguided obsession.

ISBNs, copyrights, algorithms and lists

Do You Need an ISBN?

An International Standard Book Number (ISBN) is what you see on the barcode on printed books. It's an identifier, a way for distribution channels to easily keep track of particular titles.

You don't really *need* an ISBN to self-publish in digital format (except, as of this writing, at the Apple bookstore). If you want to eventually make your book available in print form, you do need an ISBN.

ISBN numbers can be purchased individually, book by book, or in a batch. Self-publishing services will also offer you an ISBN option.

But you can always add an ISBN later.

To purchase ISBNs, I suggest doing so in lots of ten, and through Bowker at their website:

http://www.myidentifiers.com.

Note: having an ISBN is not the same as having a registered copyright.

Do You Need to Register Your Copyright?

When a writer writes something, he owns the copyright immediately. There is no registration requirement for this.

What registering your copyright with the Copyright Office in Washington, D.C. does is give you a legal leg to stand on if you ever are in the position of wanting to sue someone for copyright infringement.

The Copyright Office puts it this way in their FAQ: "Registration is recommended for a number of reasons. Many choose to register their works because they wish to have the facts of their copyright on the public record and have a certificate of registration. Registered works may be eligible for statutory damages and attorney's fees in successful litigation. Finally, if registration occurs within 5 years of publication, it is considered prima facie evidence in a court of law."

Go to www.copyright.gov for information and registration info.

The Mystery of the Algorithm

You'll hear a lot of talk about algorithms on indie websites. Simply put, an algorithm is a set of rules in the DNA of a system designed to result in certain outcomes.

Thus, it is as complicated as DNA itself. Which means you don't have to understand them to live, just know they exist and don't do things to damage them.

In ebook terms, the algorithm is what online booksellers, like Amazon and Barnes & Noble, use to direct readers to other books they might like to buy.

It's a function of up-selling.

So, one way an algorithm might work is to suggest to a reader who bought a thriller other, similar thrillers the reader might enjoy.

Which books are selected as suggestions is determined by the particular algorithm used by the seller. Which is a secret. And can be changed without notice.

Your job is to avoid placing impediments in the way of a healthy algorithm.

You do that by, guess what, writing great books that generate word of mouth.

You choose the right categories and tags for your books.

Lists, Lists and More Lists

If you want to get obsessive, if you want to become Ahab chasing after the White Whale of popularity, then start trying to understand and game the various lists. Lists on Amazon, like bestseller lists, specialized-bestseller lists and popularity lists (not the same things).

Try to figure out what the algorithms are for each. And when they change, which they will, stay up for 48 hours straight trying to figure it all out again.

Or don't.

Instead, keep following Law #2 and make your life simple. Let the lists take care of themselves. Which they will, if you write good books.

What About DRM?

Digital Rights Management (DRM) is a way to limit the use of content on a particular device. The main idea is to prevent illegal copying and distributing of an ebook once it's purchased for an e-reader.

DRM has a long and contentious history. Originally touted as a way to avoid piracy, it is thought by many to simply be a reader inconvenience.

On the piracy issue, some indie authors feel that by selling books at a reasonable price in trusted online stores, the fears are largely moot. There is anecdotal data to suggest that sales might actually go up, marginally, with a DRM-free offering that is pirated.

Anyway, the weight of opinion seems to be: don't do it.

Formatting

"When it comes to e-books, formatting is everything," says Steven Booth of Genius Book Company. "Without clean formatting (e.g., using indents rather than tabs), the manuscript simply won't translate into an e-book well and probably won't look very nice at all."

Formatting is about making the reading experience smooth and effortless for the reader. You have two choices:

1.   You can do it yourself.

2.   You can farm it out.

You can learn to produce books properly formatted for the various online stores. But it will take time and training. You'll have to learn about using styles in Word and font sizes and scene breaks and optional hyphenation and so on. You'll have to check each format to make sure it shows up properly on an e-reader.

You also need to know how to create a clickable Table of Contents. "A hyperlinked table of contents," says Booth, "allows the user to jump to the table of contents, and then jump to whatever part of the book they want. It creates a much better user experience."

K. A. Hitchens of Booknook.biz has an excellent checklist of what to watch out for in preparing a Word document for formatting. You can find it at:

http://crimefictioncollective.blogspot.com/2012/05/dozen-dos-and-donts-on-prepping-your.html
–Crime Fiction Collective

If you'd rather not bother with learning how to do it yourself, you can find plenty of services that will do the conversions for you at a reasonable cost. Compare prices, get recommendations and be prepared to book a job several weeks in advance.

The more complex your book (i.e., with graphics and links) the more complicated the formatting process. But note, for fiction, so called "enhanced" books (those that include all sorts of clickable bells and whistles) have not yet caught on in a big way. Readers, it seems, still want a story without distraction.

For those producing books which rely on more immersive experiences, e.g. non-fiction and children's, you will need specialized help.

Again, spend time researching the field. Google "ebook formatting services" and you'll get plenty of hits.

Covers

In the past, self-published books were printed either by companies the author contracted with or via "vanity publishers." The latter were one-stop services that charged huge dollars so the author could proudly hold up a completed book. It was mainly "vanity" because the books almost always sat unsold in boxes in the garage.

And had cheesy looking covers.

It was hard to do quality print covers. It was easy to do cheesy.

Today, with all the design software available, a graphic artist can do a superb cover in almost no time.

The ease of the process, however, has tempted some authors to rush into digital with covers that are, well, not exactly ready for prime time.

Take a look at the following book cover and list everything you think is wrong with it. I'll wait.

How many things did you find wrong with it?

Let's start with the footprint. It's *square.* Now there is no reason why it can't be. There is no law that says books have to have another aspect ratio besides square.

But we are still in an age when everyone is used to a certain way books look: they are taller than they are wide.

When people see a square cover it reminds them of a CD (remember those?).

Next, the drawing looks like it was done in a few minutes at Starbucks by someone who was bored and wanted to sketch a person at the next table.

The fonts are standard and not compelling.

Do you see anything else?

It's that little word "by." Legitimate book covers never have that. Check out traditionally published books and you'll see.

The point being, your covers need to replicate the look of a quality, traditionally published book.

Now take a look at the real thing, as rendered by Premier Digital Publishing:

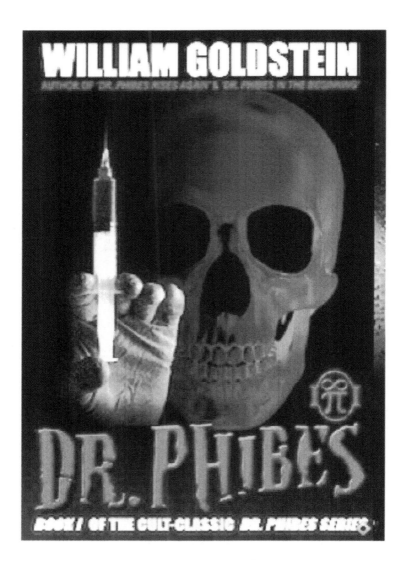

The differences are obvious. This looks like a real book. It has gripping art that captures the exact tone of the story. The font for the title is also in keeping with the book's feel.

There's also a little symbol attached. That's because this book is the first of a series of Dr. Phibes books to be republished. Each subsequent book use the same template, but changes the cover image. Thus, when lined up, a reader can easily identify the series books.

So . . . do not go hastily into cover design. I strongly advise you to seek out cover design services or individual artists.

A fair price range for a cover is $100 - $300, unless you have highly specialized requirements and engage someone who can deliver.

One midlist writer of some note, converting to digital, paid an artist $2,000 for a cover. What was produced was a professionally looking cover . . . that could have been had for $200. In other words, it was not so over and above in quality that it justified a 10x markup.

Another author decided to try his hand at designing his own covers. He found a cool photograph online that was perfect. He contacted the photographer to see what sort of licensing could be worked out. The photographer wanted $1,000.

The author then went to iStockphoto.com and found a similar image that cost $45 for a license.

There's the old saying, *You get what you pay for.*

In digital cover design, *You don't get what you overpay for.*

If you are a hearty soul who does want to try doing cover design, at least do the following:

    a. Study many traditionally designed covers in your genre.

    b. Start a portfolio of the covers you like the best.

    c. Look for simple design consistencies.

    d. Become conversant with fonts.

    e. Become conversant with design. (One good source is Robin Williams, *The Non-Designers Design Book)*

    f. Make sure your cover looks good as a thumbnail.

    g. Make sure your cover conveys the tone of your book.

If you want to hire a cover designer (a good choice) then compare the services of several, and do the following:

    a. Give them an idea of how you want the cover to look. You do this by going on Amazon or Barnes & Noble and looking for covers in your genre. You collect a number of these that resonate with you and put them into a PDF to send to your designer.

    b. Provide the cover artist with your elevator pitch.

c. Ask for a deal that includes at least a revision and a polish. You use the revision to clear up any misconceptions or things you don't like. The polish is the fine-tuning aspect. Try to negotiate this as part of the fee.

d. If you have several books being readied, ask the cover designer for a package deal and a discount.

Design Laws for Print Runs

I remember one eager young author running up to me with his newly printed book! He'd had a cover artist do the cover and all the rest he did himself.

"It was easy!" he crowed. "Look!"

I took the book and casually flipped through it.

And pegged it immediately as an amateur job, with at least four design mistakes running through it.

It is here that I bring up my theory of the "speed bumps." When I teach writing technique, I sometimes refer to "rules of the road." That is, things that every writer of fiction (or in some cases, non-fiction) should do.

And when I do, I'll get a protest voice or two, saying, "There *are* no rules!"

At which point I sigh, shake my head, and set the writer (figuratively) on my knee.

Because when you ignore the "rules," you may not have a reader sitting there analyzing the mistake, but you do create a speed bump. Something jolts the reader, even at a subconscious level, out of a deep, immersive experience.

As an example, compare these two passages:

Dagwood was really upset with Mary. He was angry. So angry he thought he might do something violent.

Dagwood's throat clenched. He picked up the chair and threw it at Mary's head.

The first is what we call in the fiction trade "telling." The second is "showing." For such an emotional moment, the second is obviously preferred. It puts us right there in the scene, creating feeling inside us.

The first example communicates information, but it creates a speed bump. The reader is brought out of the optimum reading experience.

Which brings us back to the design rules for a print book. Readers might not know what they are with certainty, but when they see them violated some distant alarm goes off in their brain that says, "Amateur."

One simple example is the blank page with a page number on it.

Go look for these things in a professionally designed and traditionally published book. On second thought, don't waste your time, because you won't find them.

So . . . when you get ready to design your immortal print classic, don't hurt it by throwing in a bunch of speed bumps.

Follow the rules of the road:

- Odd pages go on the right side

- No running heads (a "header" at the top of the page) on chapter openings

- Begin new chapters on odd numbered (right side) pages

- Don't have a blank page on the right

- Don't put page numbers or running heads on blank pages

- Use a standard print serif font (e.g., Garamond, Book Antiqua; Times and Times New Roman are old newspaper fonts, not good for print book look; sans serif fonts like Helvetica are harder to read but can be used for chapter titles, etc.)

- Use justified margins, not "ragged right"

- Get the front and back matter right (follow the design of traditionally printed books)

Get to understand these by studying many different traditionally published books. It won't be long at all before you know the rules well. You could even pass a driving test.

Print on Demand (POD)

As with digital publishing in general, you have options. You can do it all yourself or hire out the work.

Then you set up an account with a Print on Demand (POD) service, like Lightning Source or CreateSpace.

Then you get to figure out how to sell those books.

At least you don't have to do a print run of 3,000, as in days of old, and end up with a garage full of books.

Still, it's nice to have access to print runs for speaking engagements--especially if you are a non-fiction author. Selling books at the back of the room is a longstanding way to make extra income for speakers on specific subjects.

Don't Overlook Audio Books

There is some data to suggest that much reading in the near future will move to audio. Regardless of the trend, certainly having audio books available for purchase is another stream of income for your work.

And that's what makes for long-term success: the streams. As of this writing, I have contracted to bring my first ebook, *Watch Your Back,* to audio via ACX.com. That is a service that makes it ridiculously simple to make your books available to a listening readership.

Unless you have the voice and training for it, and the right equipment, don't try narrating the book yourself. Instead, via ACX, audition potential voices. You upload a sample and put out the word and wait for the audio responses.

Once you have selected a narrator, you work out the financial arrangement. You can pay up front for the production and own the rights completely, or do a 50-50 royalty split with the producer/narrator.

Which is better? Naturally, if you can pay up front, you keep all the income. But know this: a quality narrator can cost you $2,000 or more for a full length book recording. But you get what you pay for. You want a quality narrator. It's the most important aspect, of course, so you do not want to shirk.

You should adapt the cover of your book, which is in book size dimensions, to a square cover. Keep the same design so people will connect it with the book.

All the information is on the ACX website. And since your book is already written, the ROI on this aspect of your platform is going to be relatively high.

Law #4: You Must Develop and Work a Marketing Plan

Okay, now you've got a book ready to go.

Congratulations.

Who's going to buy it?

How are you going to let the world know it's there?

This is where you need a marketing plan that is more than "I'll Tweet about it five times a day for a month." (Which is a bad plan. More on that below).

The buzz word is "discoverability," and the challenge is there is an ever-increasing sea of people wanting their books discovered. How will you compete with that?

You take it to market, remembering the following axiom: Only 20% of marketing works and we don't know which 20%.

That's a bit cynical but there is a grain of truth in it. There is no sure-fire marketing plan, no one-size-fits-all method of getting the word out.

The important thing is that you *do* plan and you *work the plan* and you *make adjustments along the way*.

A complete coverage of marketing ideas is beyond the scope of this book. You can find an endless barrage of anecdotal evidence and advice on the subject. Here I will give you a starter plan to get you going. It's basic and it's workable for any schedule.

Your marketing plan will consist of at least:

1. A pricing strategy

2. Social media presence

3. Newsletter/email program

4. Reviews, interviews and guest blogging

Pricing strategy

Right now the online stores and distribution services give independent authors the lion's share of the income from a book.

Amazon, for example, gives an author 70% of the net from books priced between $2.99 and $9.99. It's *net* because there are delivery charges. It costs to deliver a book electronically via a digital network. Amazon passes that cost along to the authors. Currently that charge is $0.15 per MB.

Thus, your "take home" on a book that is 1 MB or less, and priced at $2.99, is 70% of $2.99 – .15 ($2.84) = $1.99.

On the matter of pricing your ebooks, there is no consensus and a lot of anecdotes. Remember the admonition: everyone's mileage will vary.

When ebooks really started to take off, 99¢ and $2.99 were the dominant price points. Amanda Hocking and John Locke are two authors who tore it up early on, using a 99¢ strategy with series books.

Both authors used their popularity to land large contracts from traditional houses.

Opinions vary on the efficacy of such a strategy today as a way to make significant income.

Some believe that perceived value is taking hold with consumers, and that 99¢ is starting to be seen as a less attractive option.

Others say it is still a good way to get new readers, and advocate a "low-high" approach, where some of your offerings are at the low end, to entice new readers into the fold.

Part of the decision depends on how many books you have available. If, for example, you are doing a series, you might price them at $3.99 but offer the first for 99¢, either permanently or for "a limited time only" as an inducement to get people signed onto the series.

There are many, many ways to structure a balanced "low-high" strategy.

There is also something to be said for a "menu" approach that prices by length, for example:

Short stories (under 15k words) – 99¢
Novelette (around 16 – 22k) - $1.49
Novella (23 – 50k) - $2.99
Novels - > 50k - $2.99 - $3.99

Non-fiction prices require some further thought. People read certain non-fiction titles expecting to find information that will be helpful to them in some way. If that is valuable information, they can be expected to pay a little more.

But remember, the bestselling non-fiction writers are those who have a platform and are able to connect with a targeted audience.

If you are writing on a subject you're passionate about, but don't have a "name" yet, you would do well to build your platform (which includes selling your ebook) by making yourself and your books available at lower prices — until you gain more reach.

And guess what? All of the above is malleable and subject to change. But that shouldn't be news to you. Everything in the publishing world right now is subject to change.

My advice: settle on a strategy first, perhaps using the above menu, and experiment a little at a time. Keep abreast of the discussions of pricing strategies on various blogs.

What About Free?

And then there is the matter of giving away free books. As of this writing, that is something available to authors who publish with the Kindle Select program. In return for being exclusive with Amazon for a 90-day period (renewable) the author can offer a book for free for five days, divided up however he chooses. (This program is subject to change, so check for updates).

Some authors are very happy for the exposure and possible "bump" in actual sales.

Other authors think consumers are wary of FREE now, and the return (measured by new readers) is not worth it.

Still others see a lot of free books as creating buzz and generating future readers.

Others simply don't like exclusivity.

Once again, there is no hard or fast rule here. Evidence is

pretty much anecdotal. You can always give it a shot and measure your own results. Using Kindle Select is best, in my opinion, when you have at least three or four other titles available for sale. Then you can get a feeling for the "bounce."

Social Media

By social media I mean anything that you can do online for free that connects you with actual and potential readers. Oh yeah, and keeps you from suffering SMA: *social media anxiety.*

Shortly after the launch of my ebooks I started getting emails from author friends, some of whom are flummoxed or annoyed about the whole social media marketing thing. These are established writers who feel pressure to Tweet this and Facebook that, and blog the other thing. All of which takes time away from what they want to do most — write fiction.

And then there are the newbies, who are being told *You have to have a platform* even before you have a book, which always seems like telling a Sea Scout he has to build a boat before he can go to the beach.

It's a real concern, because too much stress and attention put on self-promotion and marketing can actually have an adverse affect on your writing, and even your personal life. On the other hand, an author does need to get in the game in *some* way.

So what's the balance? What follows are tips for getting a

foothold in social media marketing. They seem to work for me, so do with them what you will.

1. Specialize

Don't try to be active on every possible platform. You'll end up diluting your effectiveness in each. Instead, choose two or three and get really good at it.

For me, it's primarily blogging (at The Kill Zone) and Twitter. I find the substance of blogging once a week, and the real time of Twitter each day, the perfect blend. On occasion I drop into other blogs and comment if I feel I have something to add to the discussion. I do have a Facebook author page.

I do an occasional video about writing.

The smartest social media guy I know, Thomas Umstattd of Author Tech Tips, says, "It is much better to specialize. Seth Godin does not do Twitter or Facebook. He just has the most popular blog ever. Be faithful in a few areas and then you will be ready to be faithful in many areas."

2. Don't Be Like Alec Baldwin in Glengarry Glen Ross

Remember the famous Glengarry Glen Ross speech delivered by Alec Baldwin? "ABC – Always Be Closing!" The hard sell, all the time.

Not in social media. If it's always about you and your books, it gets tiresome fast. You may think you're doing a numbers game, like sales folk, who cold call with the same script over and over until they land a fish.

In social media, the key word is "social" as in "relating to or designed for activities in which people meet each other for beneficial exchange."

Don't be repetitive, sending the same tweet or message over and over again: *Please follow me on my fan page.* Followed a day later by, *Please follow me on my fan page.* You might as well type *Apply directly to the forehead* because that's what people will want to do with the headache you've given them.

Try to give each message a unique spin or angle. You're a writer, aren't you? Prove it.

3. Use the 90/10 Rule

Spend 90% of your social media time focusing outward. Interact with people. Provide good content. Link to other sites and articles of value. Be personable. Make people glad they have you on their list of people to read.

Use only 10% of the time to "sell" something. And even when you do, don't make it a generic "Buy my stuff" (BMS) kind of thing. If you do BMS over and over again, people are going to tire of you and find ways to avoid your posts.

Instead, always provide some sort of *reason* people should buy your stuff. Maybe it's the launch, which you can announce winsomely and with a little panache. Or a contest. Or you're providing some proof of value (such as a clip of a review). You can be clever in how you word things. Anything but "Buy my stuff!"

4. Don't Hurt Your Writing Time or Your Life

If you find your social media presence detracting from your writing time and your ability to produce quality words, cut back. If you're on Facebook more than you're with your family, check your priorities. This stuff isn't as important as either of those two things.

5. Don't Sweat It

No one knows what works. In fact, even the stuff that works doesn't work all the time. This is a fluid and un-measurable sea we're in. So find a good balance, provide quality, be consistent and be patient.

A Note About Blogging

Richard Mabry (rmabry.blogspot.com), a traditionally published author, came to a writing career later than most, after retiring from a full time medical practice. What he was told at the beginning of his journey didn't thrill him.

"When I began writing (long before I was published), I was told I needed a "platform." Not being a very good carpenter, I was glad to hear that this was figurative, not literal. But when it came time to start my blog, I faced it with the same enthusiasm I showed for my first colonoscopy—I knew it was necessary, but that didn't make me look forward to it."

But he did start blogging, slowly, consistently. "I learned to blog the way I learned a lot of things in life — trial and error (and occasionally reading the directions). Several years and several hundred posts later, I find that it's a great way to connect with my readers. I've settled into a twice-a-week routine, with half my posts dealing with the writing life, the others talking about 'just stuff.' I've learned to just be myself, and my readers seem to like it."

Which is the key: connection with readers. Even if the readership is modest, the investment is in the future."

Jody Hedlund (http://www.jodyhedlund.com) is an author who has grown a terrific blog over a period of years. I asked for permission to share some of her tips on starting a blog:

1. Start blogging well before publication. I began blogging months before I had an agent or book contract. Thus I had plenty of time to build genuine relationships. My followers didn't have to worry that I was blogging to sell them anything.

2. Actively seek others out and mingle. I didn't sit back and wait for people to come to me. I made a point of sticking out the hand of friendship to others. I followed the links of bloggers in comments of more popular blogs I was reading (especially people whose comments indicated they might be someone I'd like to get to know). I went to their sites, started reading their posts, and took the initiative.

3. Comment regularly. Whenever I visited a blog, I tried to leave a thoughtful comment that would let the person know I was genuinely interested in what they had to say.

Over time, they would get to know me and often would come visit my blog in return.

4. Follow others generously. Most blogs I visited, I signed up to follow. I figured it was supportive to that blogger. And even if they didn't follow me back, I still was getting my name and avatar into a variety of places where others might see me and follow the link back to my blog.

5. Schedule time for visiting other blogs. During my early blogging days, I'd allot 30 minutes to an hour for reading and commenting on other blogs. After I got busier, I'd usually try to reciprocate visits to those who regularly visited me, or new visitors, or hard-core followers. The important thing was that I scheduled blog-hopping and made a point of keeping in contact with followers on a regular basis.

6. Post on your own blog consistently. I also tried to post interesting, thought-provoking, or helpful posts to my readers. I made sure people knew my schedule and I stayed consistent. I also have always kept my name, author photo, and contact information clearly visible. In other words, I've tried to maintain a professional but warm appeal to my blog.

Alternatives to Blogging

If consistent blogging seems overwhelming to you, again, don't sweat it. John Locke rose to prominence with very infrequent but highly specialized blog posts. He states: "My approach to blogging is to post approximately 12 to 15 blogs per year! That's not a misprint. I rarely write two blogs in the same month, and never write unless I have a specific purpose. I spend weeks deciding on the topic and days trying to determine the most effective way to present it, which will always amount to less than 800 words. I spend hours composing, formatting and shaping it into the best blog I can write."

But note that Locke has a strategic approach to what he blogs about. You can read more about that in his ebook *How I Sold 1 Million ebooks in 5 Months!*

Another alternative to solo blogging is to get together with a group of like-minded writers and start a group blog. One way to do this is to attend a good writers conference and meet a lot of people, see who you connect with and who seems a good match for you. This removes the burden of having you do everything on your own.

Finally, instead of blogging yourself, you can become a frequent and substantive contributor in the comments section of popular blogs. This is not a place for you to sell your books but to offer real interaction with the blogger and other commenters. If you do that, you earn trust.

And then, when your book comes out, you can politely ask the blog for a possible interview or guest blog spot.

One last note. If you are writing non-fiction and have an area of expertise, your blog can become the fodder for a book. You simply collect your blog posts on a subject and clean them up, put them in some kind of order, add additional content and pretty soon you'll have a book to sell.

I am considered an expert in writing fiction. Having the #1 bestselling fiction writing book for several years running (*Plot & Structure*) helped with credibility. When I started blogging at The Kill Zone, I naturally saw this as an opportunity to increase my production of writing helps.

After about two years, I had enough posts to create *Writing Fiction For All You're Worth.* I will be adding another, similar title soon.

Author Newsletter/Email Program

A newsletter is a popular item for many authors who have an opt-in mailing list of at least 1,000. To avoid spamming issues a service should be utilized. MailChimp (as of this writing) offers free mailings for lists under 2,000. VerticalResponse and ConstantContact offer a suite of services and pricing.

Here is the main thing you need to understand about newsletters: people don't read them.

Or, to put it another way, most author newsletters are not reader friendly.

For one thing, they may be too long. In a study conducted by EmailLabs, researchers found that readers spend an average of 15-20 seconds on emails they open.

And if there are a lot of graphics on the page, the reader is spending precious seconds bounding around on those.

Simply put, you have to be able to get them to read and

understand your copy in precious little time.

And too many graphics are distracting.

Starting with a fancy masthead. All the email services offer pre-designed templates that make it very easy for you to go nuts. Don't do that. Think of every graphic element as a potential distraction, and plan accordingly.

Even a book cover is a potential distraction. MarketingSherpa offers the following admonition: "If your email has any graphic elements aside from textual words, chances are some of the 15-20 seconds is spent looking at stuff like your logo instead of reading 50 words of your copy. What does it mean? That your customers and prospects will only give you a few seconds to convince them to act, and they are probably reading a heck of a lot less copy than you hoped."

One strategy is not to send out something that looks like a newsletter, but simply looks like an email. And a short one at that.

Your message should have one main point and one main action it calls for. If you overload the content or ask readers to do more than one thing, it dilutes the overall effectiveness of the communication.

Try this: design the essence of your message in 140 characters or less. Just like a tweet. If you can capture the single point of your message in that space, you are ready to write your copy.

And a simple way to design your copy is with the WWH formula:

What?
Why?
How?

What is the main benefit? That should go in the first line. For example, if you are offering a book for a limited time at 99¢, that's your opening:

I'm glad to be offering my cookbook, HANNIBAL LECTER'S FAVA BEAN FAVORITES, for only 99¢. But act soon.

Why gives backup to your benefit. Why should a reader care to order your book?

Now is the perfect time to create a dish your neighbors will love. As the Census Takers Union recently noted, "Hannibal Lecter is someone you ought to watch very carefully."

How is the action element.

Click here to order from Kindle or Nook or Kobo.

Then you can finish off with any relevant added content you desire: blurbs, a thank you, a further update on yourself (short). Then sign off and you're done.

Some DOs of author newslettering:

DO Keep matters short and sweet. One page.

DO ask for action.

DO spend time designing a *benefits* subject line.

Some DO NOTs of author newslettering:

DO NOT over mail. Once a month is the maximum (or they'll get annoyed with you).

DO NOT under mail. Once a quarter is minimum (or they may forget you).

DO NOT use white on black type. Too hard to read. I got one newsletter like this from a bestselling author and I could hardly read it. I passed on the book.

DO NOT use a generic subject line, such as "Thaddeus Croshaw's November Book News." (Exception: If you have a Non-fiction brand and the information is valuable to a select target group, e.g., Kim Kardashian's Marital Bliss Tips / November)

DO NOT use the words "Check out" or "FREE" in your subject line, as spam filters don't like them.

Here is an example of an author newsletter that worked for me. It's from mystery writer Dennis Palumbo. The subject line was specific:

Dennis Palumbo's "Mirror Image" is now a 99 cent ebook!

Notice how the subject line contains the benefit. It is not **Dennis Palumbo's April Book News.** That is no benefit to me. But a 99¢ book just may be. It's enough to get me to read the copy.
And here is the copy, in its entirety:

FYI, this month only, my publisher, Poisoned Pen Press, is offering my debut Daniel Rinaldi thriller, MIRROR IMAGE, as an ebook for just 99 cents!

If you haven't yet made the acquaintance of trauma expert and police consultant Dr. Dan Rinaldi, a character Kirkus Reviews calls "Jack Reacher with a psychology degree," this is your chance.

To purchase the ebook of MIRROR IMAGE at this special promotional rate, just click on this link:

[LINK]

Here's what some noted mystery authors have to say about Mirror Image:

"Using his background as a licensed psychotherapist to good advantage, Palumbo infuses his fast-moving, suspenseful story with fascinating texture, interesting characters, and the twists, turns and surprises of a mind-bending mystery. Very impressive." —Stephen J. Cannell, writer/creator of *The Rockford Files*

"Mirror Image is a rich, complex thriller, built around a sizzling love affair. A compelling read, with surprising twists and characters that leap off the page." —Bobby Moresco, Oscar-winning writer/producer of *Crash* and *Million Dollar Baby*

"Mirror Image is a deviously plotted thriller with lots of shocks and surprises you won't see coming." —Thomas Perry, Edgar-winning, New York Times best-selling crime novelist

"A debut thriller filled with action, deduction and romance, expertly paced for maximum suspense."
—Dick Lochte, award-winning author and critic

"Mirror Image is a standout mind-bender! Dennis Palumbo knows his craft. This guy can write." —Ridley Pearson, New York Times best-selling crime author

I hope you'll consider taking advantage of this special offer. Thanks! –Dennis

What I like about this is that the benefits and action call-out are at the top, in very short order. You know exactly what the offer is and how to take advantage of it. The blurbs, and they are good ones, come at the end, meaning a busy reader can skip over them if he wants to.

The heart of this email was accomplished in the first 73 words.

That is how it's done.

Subscribe to several authors' newsletters and start analyzing them. Which ones work for you, and which don't? Why? Become a student of the sales letter genre.

Targeted Emailing

The author newsletter is sent out en masse.

A targeted email is one that goes to a smaller group for a specific purpose.

For example, it's common for published authors to have a group of "influencers." These are people who have expressed interest in receiving a book and then recommending it to their own networks. Part of your strategy should be to get your book into their hands early. Yes, offer to send them a free book and ask for their help in getting the word out to their own tribes. Be sure to provide them with the link to the dedicated web page for your book (you do have one, don't you?). On this page you have your elevator pitch marketing copy and links to the various online bookstores.

So the sequence of the targeted email campaign is to:

1. Get an influencer to request your book
2. Request that they pass the information to their networks
3. Include a link to your book's web page for those in the network to access the information on your book
4. Close the sale at your web page

Reviews, Interviews and Guest Blogging

Reviews of your book, at the online stores and by book review blogs, should be sought in a systematic way.

First, identify the best blogs for possible reviews of your books. Approach these blogs with a personal email to the administrator. Don't do generic emails. Be sure you've spent actual time looking at the blog.

Second, ask your growing network of readers to consider leaving a review on Amazon and Barnes & Noble. If you get an email from someone who liked your book, thank them and ask for a review. Nicely of course. Don't make it seem like a demand or an obligation.

Offer to do an interview for a popular blog. Lay the groundwork for this by first offering some relevant comments to posts in that blog. Try to find a relevant "hook" that would make you an attractive interview subject.

For example, if the blog is dedicated to the craft of writing, your hook might be that you are self-publishing now and that craft study is part of your plan. You could offer to talk about what you're doing in that arena.

You could even offer that as a guest blogger. The way you would approach a blog administrator for this is the same way freelance writers query periodicals. You have to be that purposeful about it.

Spend a day studying the querying secrets of successful

freelance authors. A great place to start is with *The Writers Digest Guide To Query Letters* by Wendy Burt-Thomas (Writer's Digest Books)

How to Handle Negative Reviews

Every author, no matter how good, is going to get his share of negative reviews.

So keep a couple of things in mind.

The first is to remember that the greatest writers of all time have been slammed in print. Many examples of this have been collected in a wonderful little book, *Rotten Reviews* by Bill Henderson. Here are a couple of my favorites:

Thomas Bailey Aldrich, writing in the *Atlantic Monthly* in 1892, said of Emily Dickenson, "An eccentric, dreamy, half-educated recluse in an out-of-the-way New England village — or anywhere else — cannot with impunity set at defiance the laws of gravitation and grammar. Oblivion lingers in the immediate neighborhood."

Nothing of Mr. Aldrich, to my knowledge, remains in print.

The eminent Clifton Fadiman, in *The New Yorker* no less, said of Faulkner's *Absalom, Absalom!* that it was "the final blowup of what was once a remarkable, if minor, talent."

When you get a bad review, remember you're in very good company.

And then remind yourself *constantly* that you are a writer because you write. There are many more people who do not write yet feel perfectly at ease sniping at those who do. When such a snipe comes your way, remind yourself that you are the one putting yourself on the line, opening a vein, walking the tightrope, singing a solo under hot lights. You are part of a courageous bunch who are all about *doing*. Teddy Roosevelt's famous advice applies to writers:

"It is not the critic who counts: not the man who points out how the strong man stumbles or where the doer of deeds could have done better. The credit belongs to the man who is actually in the arena . . . who, at the best, knows, in the end, the triumph of high achievement, and who, at the worst, if he fails, at least he fails while daring greatly, so that his place shall never be with those cold and timid souls who knew neither victory nor defeat."

Get in the arena. Go at your writing with all the devotion and love and enthusiasm you have. When the darts of rejection or criticism come your way, keep writing.

I also like John Locke's philosophy. He believes you actually *need* to garner some negative reviews along with positives, or your writing is not original enough and you're not building a loyal fan base. "The reason you'll get some great reviews for your original writing is because I don't care what you're selling, there's a market for it! What I'm saying, if you're not offending a significant number of readers, your writing is probably not very original. And the less original your writing, the less loyal your fan base will be."

What About Paid Positioning?

You can pay people to help you market your book. The ways they attempt to do this are varied and tied to "targeting" criteria:

- Click-through ads (e.g. display, banners, Facebook)
- Blog tours
- Media buzz creation (also known as PR)
- Direct email campaigns
- Giveaways and contests

You can replicate most of these yourself but it takes a massive amount of work and expertise to keep you from throwing your money down a dark hole.

So what is the best investment for your advertising dollar? No one knows.

You'll get people who say don't do it. Others who say it's worth it to get more "eyes on your page."

There are some who measure the worth only by actual, hard numbers.

Others think it's an investment in the future.

My advice is simply this: don't go into debt. If you want to use discretionary funds to give paid positioning a try, go for it. Do your research. Get recommendations. Take baby steps.

Learning the ins and outs of marketing, what works and what doesn't, and deciding where to spend your time is all an ongoing process.

Here's the bottom line, though: don't ever let this overwhelm you. The place you should be spending your most time is with Law #2. Be a great writer. If you do that, you'll start to rise. If you ignore that, all this other stuff won't matter.

Mistakes to Avoid

You have to realize that once you are out there marketing your book, you're out there forever. What you post, tweet, publish, Facebook, pin or otherwise put out in the ether is all going into a big blender and creating a brew that is you. You need to think through everything you do before you do it.

Here are some typical mistakes I see that I pass along so you can avoid dumping carbolic acid in your blender.

1. Shooting from the hip

The temptation to spout before your think is ever present on the internet. How many times have we seen some dumb tweet completely change how we feel about someone? In some cases it's ruined a career. Google "Anthony Weiner Twitter scandal" for a notable example.
While it's true that blogs and other social media allow for venting, you are trying to create a public persona for the future. For forever. There used to be a simple adage about keeping one's mouth shut when angry or frustrated, about

"counting to ten" before saying or doing something you might regret.

Think before you hit send.

Instead of an instant tweet or Facebook post in anger, write a short letter to yourself and spout off as much as you like. Then let it sit for an hour.

2. Giving up

Sometimes all the thoughts about social media and the flood of stimuli out there can feel daunting. Like: *Who is ever going to care about anything I say or do?*

Don't chuck it. Just keep doing what you comfortably can, with quality. Remember, Law #2 is your bread-and-butter. Keep concentrating on that and just do what you can.

3. Taking yourself too seriously

If you end up making a lot of money from self-publishing, be thankful and humble about it. The temptation to start bragging about how great you're doing is ever present in the world of blogging and social media.

There is a fine art to "tooting your own horn" without being snooty about it. See #4.

4. Tooting your own horn without making music

Every writer has to do some self-promotion. Publishers and agents demand it. If you're self-publishing, you can't survive without some form of it.

Yet many authors feel uncomfortable tooting their own horns. Let me assuage that discomfort.

Self-promotion need not be "shameless," and indeed can be a benefit to all, if you remember one simple thing: the **Law of Reciprocity**. This law holds that when you offer something of value to another, they are much more likely to give something in return.

In social media, for example, the Law of Reciprocity is golden. Many an author makes the mistake of thinking social media is about marketing. In reality it's about relationships. You build those slowly, through actual engagement, and not by stringing together a bunch of posts that are little more than "buy my stuff" pleadings.

So think reciprocity. Give, and you will receive. Don't just toot your own horn, make some music with it. Remember the 90/10 rule: let 90% of your online presence be about giving something of value to others and building trust.

5. Constant negativity

Yes, controversy and a liberal use of F bombs can get your blog post noticed.

For a while.

But if you keep it up, you'll alienate more people than you'll attract. You may gather an "Amen corner" of like-minded misanthropes, but you will largely be talking (or spouting) to each other.

Ben Franklin said, "Tart words make no friends; a spoonful of honey will catch more flies than a gallon of vinegar."

Look, there's a reason he's on a $100 bill and you're not.

Law #5: You Must Repeat Over and Over For the Rest of Your Life

Control your destiny, or someone else will. —Jack Welch

Successful ebook publishing is a volume business.

Even traditional publishers and authors know this. A story in the *New York Times* (May 12, 2012) told of how bestselling, A-list authors are supplementing their output to meet an ever growing demand—but also to help sell their books with short form works. For example:

The British thriller writer Lee Child, who created the indelible character Jack Reacher, is now supplementing his hardcover books with short stories that are published in digital-only format, an increasingly popular strategy to drum up attention for the coming publication of a novel.

Mr. Child's first story, a 40-page exploration of Reacher as a teenager, was released last August, several weeks before his latest novel came out in print. On the advice of his publisher, he is planning to write another digital-only short story this summer.

"Everybody's doing a little more," said Mr. Child, who is published by Delacorte Press, part of Random House. "It seems like we're all running faster to stay in the same place."

This all translates into a simple axiom: the more books you have available, the better you'll do (so long as they are the best books you can write according to Law #2). The "long tail" of marketing means you have many boats and a rising tide to lift them all.

In its 2012 survey of self-published authors, Dave Cornford and Steven Lewis determined that half the writers made only $500 in the previous year (see Cornford and Lewis, *Not a Gold Rush,* Taleist, 2012). I suspect most of these were one-title authors.

You need more than one title. You need to keep producing. Which means you are not just a salesperson. You are a writer. And a real writer can never be defeated.

William Saroyan was a real writer, someone born with fingers fitted for a typewriter. He was a short story writer at first, then a playwright, then a novelist and finally a memoirist. He is not much talked about today, but he should be.

He wrote one of the finest collections of short stories in the

American idiom, *My Name is Aram.*

He wrote a Pulitzer Prize winning play, *The Time of Your Life* (and then famously refused the prize).

He went into a period where his plays did not play and his books did not sell. Refusing to stop, he started writing quirky memoirs, like *The Bicycle Rider in Beverly Hills* and *Sons Come and Go, Mothers Hang in Forever.*

At the end of his life he wrote surely one of the oddest memoirs ever, *Obituaries.* In it he took the annual *Variety* edition that listed all the obits of movie industry people, and he went through it alphabetically, taking each name and riffing on it. Most of the time he didn't know the person, but used the name as a jumping off point for his stream-of-consciousness reminiscences.

The chapters have no paragraph breaks or indents.

It should not be readable, but oddly, it is.

Because Saroyan was a writer who would not be defeated. He once said, "A writer who is a real writer is a rebel who never stops."

Preston Sturges was a real writer. Mainly, he was one of the greatest writer-directors in Hollywood history, and surely the finest purveyor of the screwball comedy. For a period of time he wrote and directed hit after hit after hit.

And then, suddenly, he couldn't get arrested.

He did not stop writing.

And he said, "When the last dime is gone, I'll sit on the curb with a pencil and a ten-cent notebook, and start the whole thing all over again."

So now we are in a new age where it is possible for a writer to make real bank. Most writers in the past didn't make much money at all, even if they managed to get published. A scant few ever made a living at it. Many quit or just gave up.

It'll always be a challenge, but now there's a much more even playing field. You can keep going. You can keep trying. You can keep getting better. You don't have to sit down with someone telling you you're not capable, that you should just quit, that you should go away and leave your dreams to others. You don't have to take that as long as you've got a keyboard and an imagination.

And in this way, you can never be defeated.

Are you a real writer?

Then keep writing.

And don't stop.

Ever.

ABOUT THE AUTHOR

JAMES SCOTT BELL is the author of the #1 bestseller for writers, *Plot & Structure*, and numerous thrillers, including *Deceived, Try Dying* and *Watch Your Back*. His novella *One More Lie* was the first independently published work to be nominated for a prestigious International Thriller Writers Award. Under the pen name K. Bennett, he is also the author of the Mallory Caine zombie legal thriller series, which begins with *Pay Me in Flesh*. He served as the fiction columnist for Writer's Digest magazine and has written highly popular craft books for Writer's Digest Books, including : *Revision & Self-Editing, The Art of War for Writers* and *Conflict & Suspense*.

Jim taught writing at Pepperdine University and at numerous writers conferences in the United States, Canada and Great Britain. He attended the University of California, Santa Barbara where he studied writing with Raymond Carver. He graduated with honors from the University of Southern California law school

He lives in Los Angeles. His website is:

www.JamesScottBell.com.

35637891R00080

Made in the USA
Lexington, KY
18 September 2014